Australia: A Very Short Introduction

Very Short Introductions available now:

Available soon:

For more information visit our website
www.oup.com/vsi

Kenneth Morgan

AUSTRALIA

A Very Short Introduction

OXFORD
UNIVERSITY PRESS

OXFORD
UNIVERSITY PRESS

Great Clarendon Street, Oxford ox2 6DP
United Kingdom

Oxford University Press is a department of the University of Oxford.
It furthers the University's objective of excellence in research, scholarship,
and education by publishing worldwide. Oxford is a registered trade mark of
Oxford University Press in the UK and in certain other countries

British Library Cataloguing in Publication Data

Data available

Library of Congress Cataloging in Publication Data

Data available

ISBN 978-0-19-958993-7

Printed in Great Britain
on acid-free paper by
Ashford Colour Press Ltd, Gosport, Hampshire

Contents

List of illustrations

List of maps

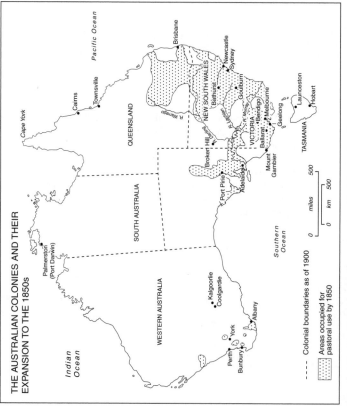

Map 1. The Australian colonies and pastoral settlement to the 1850s

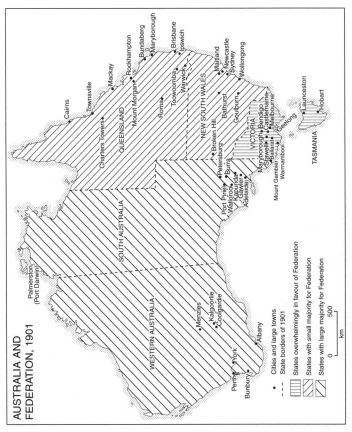

Map 2. Australia and Federation, 1901

Chapter 1
The making of Australia

Time was when an introduction to the making of Australia was unproblematic: the modern story of Australia began with James Cook claiming New South Wales for Britain in 1770 and the British convict settlement at Sydney Cove in 1788. Aborigines were omitted from the story. Thus, Walter Murdoch's school text *Making of Australia: An Introductory History* (1917) argued that 'when people talk about "the history of Australia" they mean the history of the white people who have lived in Australia', for the Aborigines 'have nothing that can be called history'. W. K. Hancock's *Australia* (1930) began with the Younger Pitt's government selecting New South Wales as a convict settlement and the emergence of the pastoral industry down under. When the book was reprinted in 1961, Hancock admitted that inattention to Aborigines showed that it had fallen behind the times. Remnants of an older attitude lingered on into the 1970s as, for example, in F. K. Crowley's remark about why a book he edited on Australia's history minimized Aboriginal affairs:

> People complain I've not put enough in about Aborigines: that's not a complaint, to me that's a simple observation. It means they've got the message. Our message is that the Aborigines were not important in the early history of white settlement.

Such a viewpoint is now marginal because of greater awareness of the Indigenous past and its contribution to Australia's history. On the other hand, modern Australia's institutions, economy, and political and social life are indelibly interwoven with the process of colonization and conquest that began in 1788. Aboriginal and European contributions to the development of Australia must therefore be considered in tandem.

This short introductory account of Australia pays attention to the longevity of settlement on the world's largest island continent, stretching back for millennia before Europeans set foot in the Antipodes, while providing a balanced account of major forces that have shaped Australian development since the Europeans arrived. This entails considering Aboriginal life, the impact of British and Irish settlement, and the more recent efflorescence of Continental European, Asian, and American influences upon Australia. The aim here is to summarize contentious topics judiciously. Positive achievements in the establishment of a relatively peaceful middling-size democracy need to be weighed against unresolved social and political matters for all Australians. But any understanding of Australia first requires some basic knowledge about its geography, climate, and people.

Natural and human resources

Australia's natural and human resources have shaped its socioeconomic environment in distinctive ways. During the last Ice Age, Australia was a larger land mass than today, known as Sahul, which incorporated Papua New Guinea and Tasmania. The land bridge across Torres Strait between southern New Guinea and the Cape York peninsula – the northernmost point in Australia – was submerged by rising sea levels more than 8,000 years ago, leading to the creation of a new continent. Modern Australia is the world's smallest, flattest, and driest continent. One of the seven largest countries in the world, it covers an area of 3 million square miles. It extends 2,500 miles from east to west and

1,800 miles from north to south. Though plains dominate Australia's landscape, mountains are found in the Southern Alps in New South Wales (notably Mount Koscziusko, 7,328 feet above sea level, one-quarter of the height of Mount Everest) and in Tasmania, which, although generally low-lying, has 50 mountains over 3,936 feet.

Australia's predominantly dry climate, especially in the vast interior open spaces, stems from limited rainfall and many days of persistent hot temperatures above 30 degrees Celsius. The last ten years, in fact, have been Australia's warmest decade on record. Half of Australia is arid, about one-fifth is desert, and one-third of its land mass receives less than 10 inches of annual rainfall. Much of Australia's soil is of poor quality for agricultural development. Desert is common in Western Australia and the Northern Territory. The Kimberley Tableland in the Western Plateau, for example, comprises 150,000 square miles of thin soils, rocky outcrops, desert and semi-desert land unsuitable for human habitation. Droughts are common in Australia, and can last for years. They mainly stem from the El Niño effect, whereby changes in ocean and atmospheric circulation lead to a negative southern oscillation that causes drought. The worst drought lasted between 1895 and 1902 and caused acute problems at a time of economic depression. Between 1997 and 2010, the Melbourne area experienced its longest drought on record. Parts of Western Australia are currently suffering higher than normal aridity from very low levels of rainfall. Bushfires are an ever-present hazard for Australians in rural communities. Water shortage will remain an acute problem in the future. Tropical North Queensland and the coastal areas of the Northern Territory are exceptions to the norm: they have a humid, monsoonal climate in summer months. Unexpected heavy rainfall can occur, such as the extensive floods that devastated much of southern Queensland in 2011, caused by a combination of the El Niño effect and the annual monsoonal low pressure trough that brings wet weather to the region.

Australia's isolation as a continent has led to a distinctive flora, fauna, and wildlife, but these have changed a great deal over many centuries. Australia once had far more forest and woodland than it has today. The Aboriginal custom of firestick foraging burned spinifex, cleared bushland for walking, eliminated less desirable plants and helped to produce habitats for animals and insects and the spread of bush tucker; but it also burned plentiful timber resources. Overstocking of animals by settlers and rabbit plagues left bare, sandy landscapes in the outback. Giant emus and large kangaroos, as fossil remains indicate, once inhabited Australia; and many species of flora and fauna have become extinct. Bush areas are common, such as the densely wooded Blue Mountains to the west of Sydney, the tropical Daintree rainforest in northern Queensland, and tracts of cool temperate rainforest in Tasmania. Nevertheless, large tranches of inland Australia comprise mile after mile of uninhabited flat land. A modern traveller exploring the outback might well imagine that Australia is an empty continent. The most common flora found in Australia are the many species of wattle and eucalypt. In the desert, small wooded clumps of spinifex are often the only visible signs of plant life. Australia's animals include types of venomous snakes, dingoes, kangaroos and wallabies, wombats, koala bears, cassowaries, Tasmanian devils, and duckbill platypuses which are only found in Australia.

Australia's population and economy reflects these geographical and climatic facts as well as the process of Aboriginal and settler use of the land. Archaeological evidence indicates that Aborigines have lived in Australia for at least 60,000–70,000 years, and possibly for over 100,000 years. Only China, Java, East Africa, and parts of the Middle East have revealed traces of human life before that time. Aborigines were once plentiful in Australia: in 1788, it is claimed, their numbers were between 600,000 and 1 million. This ancient group of people lived semi-nomadically, moving from one fertile area to another along river valleys and near coastal plains throughout Australia. Aborigines had no sense of individual ownership of land. They believed the land was sacred and that the rocks, gullies, trees, and shrubs contained ancestral spirits. One such site is Uluru (formerly Ayer's Rock) in the Northern Territory – the most familiar Aboriginal landscape symbol throughout the world.

Aborigines survived by gathering food on a daily basis. Men generally hunted for meat, while women combined their roles as mothers with gathering insects, fruits, seeds, nuts, berries, and small game. Collective practices, such as sharing food resources, were common. Aborigines controlled their population in relation to sustainable resources by infanticide when mothers already had one suckling baby. They eschewed settled agriculture partly because of the uncertainty of rainfall in Australia. Though connections existed between different groups, there was no Aboriginal nation. Indigenous people spoke a variety of languages, with different dialects, but neighbouring language users could communicate with each other. In the late 18th century, there were at least 350 distinct Aboriginal languages. Aborigines had an oral culture. They also had a sign language counterpart of their spoken language. This was used particularly at times when speech taboos were observed between kin or during mourning rites and male initiation ceremonies. Aborigines have left paintings and have passed down memories from generation to generation, but they had no written culture.

The contrast with Australia's white settlers could hardly be greater. Europeans first came to Australia many centuries after Aborigines had already lived there. Transplanted Europeans had deeply held notions of private property, of settled agriculture, of domination of the land, of expansion into new territory, of possessing land as part of an empire, and of national rivalry. Settlers had an extensive print culture to write down laws, orders, and treaties. They had a strong strain of individual acquisitiveness and, unlike the Aborigines, no spiritual connections with the land. Most settlers clustered near the coastline, especially in the southeastern part of the continent. Nearly half of Australia's modern population (9 million out of 22 million) lives in Sydney and Melbourne, which are the focal points of the most populous states – New South Wales and Victoria. In Western Australia, South Australia, and Queensland, urban centres are more scattered from one another and quite isolated. Perth, for example, is 1,672 miles by road from the nearest large city, Adelaide, making the West Australian capital one of the world's most isolated cities. Australia, then, is a land of varied geography and climate; but its natural barriers to human habitation caution against any simplistic notion that it could support a much larger population.

Discovering and possessing Australia

Aborigines had an intimate knowledge of Australia's landscape for centuries before white settlement, but their dispersion, fragmentation, and non-expansionist nature meant their cartographic knowledge did not extend throughout the continent. Aborigines had no collective impetus to possess the continent or to disseminate their local knowledge to the wider world. Europeans, on the contrary, had a long-standing curiosity about the possible vast land that lay somewhere in the southern hemisphere, and eventually this involved the thrust towards imperial possession. Terra Australis Incognita – the unknown southern land – formed part of the imaginative world of philosophers and geographers from ancient times onwards. Greek and Roman philosophers thought that, in theory, such a land must exist. In AD 150–160, Ptolemy had named a large expanse of land on the map *Terra Australis*. The 5th-century Roman philosopher Macrobius thought the Earth was divided into three climatic zones, with a large continent covering most of its southern hemisphere.

Some mapmakers later included a land mass in southern oceans without knowing its shape or extent. The 16th-century Flemish cartographers Mercator and Ortelius included such a land on their maps. The accounts of explorers complemented theoretical geography. In the 13th century, Marco Polo gathered tales from China about a great land of riches in the southern hemisphere. During the Middle Ages, the Indians, Greeks, Chinese, and Arabs all wrote about a realm somewhere to the south of Java, embellishing their accounts with stories of palaces of gold and fabulous birds of prey. But none of these speculations were verified.

Locating Terra Australis in practice resulted from the activities of Western European trading powers in the era between Columbus's discovery of America in 1492 and the French revolutionary and Napoleonic wars of 1793–1815. During that long period, Australia was found piecemeal by European voyagers. It was the last of the world's habitable continents to be explored by Europeans. That it took so long to encompass Australia stemmed from incomplete knowledge of the vast Pacific Ocean and of Australia's geography. Covering one-third of the total area of the globe and equal to all the land masses of the world put together, large expanses of the Pacific were uncharted or unmapped by Europeans until the late 18th century. Many navigators before the 17th century did not have the resources or national backing to explore the Pacific. In addition, geographical knowledge about Australia was often fragmentary and speculative before c. 1800.

Portuguese navigators may have undertaken a secret voyage of discovery to Australia between 1521 and 1524, but this is not confirmed. French charts known as the 'Dieppe maps' concerning the voyage depict a continent in the southern hemisphere named Java la Grande; but the iconography on the maps is based on Sumatran animals and ethnography, not on Australian reality, and the maps are composites of mariners' charts. Spanish interest in Australia yielded few results. Alvaro de Mendana set out from Spanish Peru in 1567 on a voyage to the southwest Pacific and reached the Solomon Islands. He made a second voyage in 1595, on which he discovered the Marquesas Islands. In 1605–6, the Portuguese navigator Pedro Fernandez de Quiros sailed across the Pacific from Peru to reach the New Hebrides. But though these voyagers hoped to find a mainland in the South Pacific, they did not sail far enough in a southwesterly direction to sight Australia. In 1606, Luis Vaez de Torres sailed through the strait that now bears his name, to the north of Australia, but his course lay near to the New Guinea coast: he did not locate the Australian mainland. These were scattered and isolated voyages because neither of the Iberian powers had a major incentive to discover Australia.

The Dutch played a more important role in the European discovery of Australia. The founding of the Dutch East India Company (the VOC) in 1602 led to voyages to the Indonesian archipelago in search of gold and spices, and from Java it was possible to proceed southwards in search of further riches. Sailing from the Netherlands to the East Indies on a 20-metre-long vessel, the *Duyken*, Willem Janszoon touched at New Guinea and the Cape York peninsula in 1606. This is the first indisputable evidence that a European had landed in Australia. Abel Janszoon Tasman made two voyages, in 1642 and 1644, to determine whether Australia (which he named New Holland) was part of a larger southern land. On the first voyage, he discovered and named Van Diemen's Land – modern Tasmania – but his attempts to land there were thwarted by rough seas and by his crew fearing they might encounter giants. Tasman sailed around the south and east parts of Van Diemen's Land, but he did not circumnavigate it and did not realize it was an island. The second voyage was devoted to mapping and charting the northwest Australian coast. Tasman's voyages failed to discover a promising new area for trade or a suitable shipping route for VOC vessels to follow in the Pacific. The regular route for the VOC took ships east across the Indian Ocean. Landfalls by these vessels on Australia's western coast became quite common by the later 17th century. The last major Dutch voyage to Terra Australis, led by Willem Hesselsz de Vlamingh in 1696, yielded disappointing results: he touched near modern Fremantle, in southwest Australia, sailed northwards to the North West Cape, and then abandoned further exploration.

Changing European attitudes towards the human and natural world gave a higher priority to Pacific exploration during the 18th century. Educated observers became more interested in mankind in its uncivilized state. Scientific curiosity gave impetus to botanical and zoological discoveries. Enlightenment thinking emphasized human progress via greater discovery of the globe. Western European nations sought improvement through trade and overseas settlement. Britain was at the forefront of these developments through the work of the Royal Society in London, the patronage of Sir Joseph Banks for collectors of new knowledge, and the Admiralty and Board of Longitude's interest in oceanic exploration. Practical knowledge and imaginative writing also stimulated the search for the great southern land. The buccaneer adventurer William Dampier's widely circulated account of landing in Western Australia in 1688 warned against settlement there owing to arid conditions. Dampier also made unfavourable comments about Aboriginal habits. Jonathan Swift's novel *Gulliver's Travels* (1726) about 'a person of quality in Terra Australis Incognita' depicted an exotic fictional society on an island off Australia's coast. In the 1740s, the travel writer John Campbell (copying Tasman) claimed that whoever discovered and settled Terra Australis 'will become infallibly possessed of territories as rich, as fruitful, & as capable of improvement as any that have been hitherto found, either in the East Indies, or the West'.

After the Seven Years' War, fascination spread in Europe about the location of the great southern land. The voyages of Captains Samuel Wallis and Philip Carteret (1766–9) had instructions to search for a land or lands of great extent in the southern hemisphere between Cape Horn and New Zealand. Wallis landed at Tahiti and Carteret discovered the Pitcairn Islands, but neither explorer found Australia. French naval explorers were active in Pacific waters in the later 18th century on voyages with scientific objectives. The Comte de Lapérouse led an expedition into Oceania which arrived at Botany Bay in January 1788 shortly after the First Fleet of convicts anchored there. With no orders to claim Australia for France, Lapérouse sailed away and his expedition was wrecked on reefs in the Solomon Islands. In September 1791, Rear Admiral Bruni d'Entrecasteaux sailed from France in search of Lapérouse. In the following year, he explored parts of Van Diemen's Land and southwestern Australia, but his voyage failed to find his lost compatriot and he himself died at sea of scurvy. The fate of Lapérouse's expedition remained unknown for 40 years until artefacts from the wreck of his ship were discovered on the coral atoll of Vanikoro.

James Cook had greater ambitions than these other explorers. In his own words, he wanted to sail 'farther than any other man has been before me' and 'as far as I think it is possible for man to go'. Cook intended to extend the geographical boundaries of existing knowledge. His three famous Pacific voyages (1768–80) led to a great increase in geographical and navigational information about the Pacific from Alaska to Tahiti and from New Zealand to Australia's east coast. In June 1770, on his first Pacific voyage, Cook's *Endeavour* anchored at Botany Bay, just south of modern Sydney, for eight days and eight nights. Within two months, Cook had charted part of Australia's eastern coastline and annexed Australia from latitude 38° south in the name of George III, calling it New South Wales. This occurred on Possession Island in Torres Strait (which, like Botany Bay, he named) on 22 August 1770. Cook had a more positive view of the Aborigines he encountered than Dampier, considering them 'far happier than we Europeans' in their natural state, but he had no qualms about claiming possession of Australia for Britain.

Aboriginal memory has a different view of Cook's dominant, imperialist view of the British acquisition of Australia. This is best captured by the Aboriginal philosopher Hobbles Danaiyarri, based

1. *The Landing of Captain Cook at Botany Bay in 1770*, by E. Phillips Fox (1902)

in northern Australia. In a narrative, transcribed in 1982, using Cook as a collective term, he wrote:

> You, Captain Cook, you the one bringing in new lotta man. Why didn't you give me fair go for my people?…what we call Australia, that's for Aboriginal people. But him been take it away. You been take that land, you been take the mineral, take the gold, everything. Take it up to this Big England.

Cook and later explorers acted as expansionist Europeans were accustomed, without taking into account Aboriginal views.

Cook's mapping and charting of Australia's east coast was extended by other explorers. Matthew Flinders discovered Bass Strait with his friend George Bass in 1798–9, thereby proving that Van

Diemen's Land was an island off mainland Australia. Then, in *H.M.S. Investigator*, Flinders led a British-backed circumnavigation of the Australian coast between December 1801 and June 1803, being the first naval explorer to do so. Flinders charted much of Australia's coast and named innumerable capes, coves, and peninsulas. He was particularly fascinated by the Indigenous people and landscape of the Gulf of Carpentaria. Some parts of the Victorian and South Australian coasts were also charted by a rival French expedition led by Nicolas Baudin that overlapped with Flinders' voyage. Unlike the British, however, the French did not settle in Australia. Just before his death in 1814, Flinders published *A Voyage to Terra Australis*, in which his maps and charts of the continent he called Australia appeared. Between 1818 and 1822, Philip Parker King, on four voyages, completed the charting of the northwestern Australian coast that Flinders had foregone owing to the leaky condition of his ship on its circumnavigatory voyage.

By the 1820s, the main contours and features of the Australian coastline were known and recorded. The interior of Australia, however, remained relatively unknown: the Blue Mountains were first crossed in 1813, but exploring the outback proved daunting. Charles Sturt led three expeditions into the interior to search for an inland sea. In 1828–9, he traced streams that carried their waters south to a greater river, the Darling, which he discovered. This demonstrated that western flowing waters in New South Wales were not an inland sea. Their ultimate destination remained unknown until Sturt's second expedition of 1829–30 established the course of the Murray River, finding, with disappointment, that its mouth comprised sandbars and lagoons through which shipping could not pass. Sturt's third expedition in 1844 ranged through New South Wales and South Australia in search of Australia's centre, but Sturt contracted scurvy and his exploring party had to be rescued. Other inland explorations also took their human toll. In 1848, the Prussian explorer and naturalist Ludwig Leichhardt disappeared while trying to cross the continent from east to west in an overland expedition funded by private subscription. In 1860–1, Robert O'Hara Burke and William John Wills, supported by donations, led an expedition of 19 men from Melbourne to the Gulf of Carpentaria, a journey of 2,000 miles from south to north. But after completing this successfully, 7 men died on the return journey at Cooper's Creek, partly because of beriberi. Only one of their party arrived back in Melbourne. Despite its loss of life, the expedition proved finally that Australia had no inland sea.

The convict legacy

White settlement in Australia began in an unusual way. It comprised a fleet of 11 vessels carrying convicts exiled from Britain for crimes, accompanied by naval officers, surgeons, marines, wives, transport seamen, and a few civilians. Captain Arthur Phillip was the commander. The vessels left Portsmouth on 13 May 1787 and reached Sydney harbour on 26 January 1788 (now celebrated as Australia Day). This was probably the only founding of a colony in modern history based primarily on a population of convicts. The British government set up such a settlement primarily because it needed a far-flung place of exile for felons. Transportation had been an important secondary punishment for decades. A parliamentary act of 1718 had sanctioned such traffic to North America: over 50,000 British and Irish convicts were sent to the tobacco colonies of Virginia and Maryland before 1776. Britain's loss of her North American colonies halted the trade. Convicts were then confined in England on old prison warships known as hulks, but the end of the American revolutionary war led to a search for a new outlet for their dispatch. Various possible destinations were found wanting, including Das Voltas Bay in West Africa. In August 1786, the Younger Pitt's government decided to exile convicts to New South Wales.

Historians have long debated whether commercial, naval, or strategic motives accompanied the plan to dump convicts. Certainly, Pitt's government was aware of commercial possibilities for the East India Company through a settlement at Sydney. It knew about the availability of flax supplies on Norfolk Island to aid the British Navy, and had considered Sydney's strategic significance as a port to counteract Spanish or French ventures in the South Pacific. But whether these additional motives were of major significance has not been proven. It is clear, however, that between the initial order for the First Fleet to sail and its arrival in Sydney, the government had developed plans for settling New South Wales within an imperial context. Subsequent fleets of British and Irish convicts were sent to New South Wales. Felons were dispatched additionally to Van Diemen's Land from 1812 and to Western Australia from 1850. Between 1788 and 1868, over 160,000 convicts reached Australian shores, the peak period being the quarter-century after 1815. Transportation came to an end in New South Wales in 1840, in Van Diemen's Land in 1853, and in Western Australia in 1868, as views changed on the efficacy of transportation as a criminal punishment.

Popular representations of convicts, from Dickens's Magwitch in *Great Expectations* (1860–1) to Robert Hughes's bestselling *The Fatal Shore* (1987), have emphasized the colourful, grim aspects of felonry. The opening pages of Dickens's novel evoke a shady netherworld of crime. Hughes depicts convict New South Wales as a vast gaol, a gulag in the southern hemisphere. Earlier writers also dwelt upon the grand guignol aspects of convict life. James Mudie, for instance, who lived in New South Wales between 1822 and 1838 as a landowner with a convict workforce, explained that the convicts consisted of

> branches lopped for their rottenness from the tree of British freedom…whom the outraged soil of England, shuddering at their crimes, has expelled, and whom she has with just abhorrence cast forth from her shores to expiate…those offences which placed the very lives of the majority of them at her mercy.

Marcus Clarke's novel *For the Term of His Natural Life* (1874) popularized the stark, inhumane treatment of convicts. Remnants of the convict presence in Australia, such as Hyde Park Barracks in Sydney or the Port Arthur penal settlement in Tasmania, remind us of the discipline, suffering, and terror experienced by transportees.

Despite this evidence, it is important to emphasize the normative aspects of convictism in Australia. Most felons served seven-year terms for convictions based on theft, usually petty or grand larceny; a minority had terms of fourteen years or life. They were invariably lower-class people who for the most part had stolen in hard times rather than people who habitually resorted to crime. Notions of convicts as a criminal class are inaccurate. Few transportees were guilty of rape, murder, or manslaughter. A minority were political dissidents. They included exiles from Ireland after the 1798 Irish rebellion and sympathizers with political radicalism in the 1830s, such as the Tolpuddle martyrs, who were sentenced to transportation after falling foul of an obscure law on swearing oaths. Most convicts were male – the ratio being four male felons to each female convict in Van Diemen's Land. Popular accounts still recirculate the myth that many female felons were depraved and prostitutes, but these attitudes were more reflective of moral condemnation of transported criminals common in the 19th century than reality.

Convicts provided much-needed labour for building colonial settlements in Australia. They were employed, initially by their military guards, in construction work, urban trades, and agricultural tasks such as ploughing, harrowing, or tending livestock. Skilled convicts were highly prized workers. Convicts appear to have formed a productive, efficient labour force. After a period of good conduct, they could apply to the governor for a ticket-of-leave in order to work for a wage. Convicts did not live in a gaol, nor were they separate from free subjects. Indeed, even in the early days of settlement at Sydney, convicts worked as dealers

2. A government gaol gang, Sydney, by Augustus Earle (1830)

and tradesmen and had relatively little contact with gaolers. Men and women were not separated. They were encouraged to marry and have families. Their children were born into freedom. They retained legal rights. In New South Wales, they had the right to present evidence in criminal courts. Former convicts became employers of felons still under sentence. Many convicts raised themselves up from an unpromising start in Australia to become respectable members of society. They were able to effect, in the main, a seamless transition into civilian life.

There were, to be sure, less savoury aspects of convictism. By the 1820s and 1830s, recalcitrant re-offenders were relocated to stark penal stations such as Macquarie Harbour, a lonely outpost in western Van Diemen's Land, or Norfolk Island, a tiny settlement situated 870 miles off Australia's east coast. At these places, convicts were sometimes subject to solitary confinement and their hair shaved. Convicts experienced fines, cautions, and flogging. Physical punishments and legal constraints appeared to set them apart from free society. Moral condemnation of transported felons persisted in Britain, Ireland, and Australia into the Victorian period. In Australia by the 1820s, free settlers referred to themselves as 'exclusives' to distinguish themselves from the 'emancipists' (ex-convicts) and their children, the currency lads and lasses – so called because the currency or paper money then issued was considered inferior to sterling. Social barriers sometimes existed between these groups. But these gradually eroded as people intermingled and intermarried, and as settlers could see that ex-convicts made as significant an economic contribution to colonial growth as free migrants.

The early champion of the emancipists was William Charles Wentworth in his newspaper the *Australian*, first issued in October 1824. Wentworth argued that all settlers in Australia deserved a 'fair go', an attitude that has persisted into modern Australian life. Nevertheless, the social stain associated with convicts faded slowly. English readers were told in 1864 that 'no one who has not lived in Australia can appreciate the profound hatred of convictism that obtains there'. It was not until the 1960s and 1970s that Australians willingly admitted that they had convict ancestors, such was the shame attached to the nation's origins. Nowadays, however, to claim a convict as an ancestor carries little stigma. Today's visitors to Sydney's Rocks can see the physical place, and perhaps grasp something of the atmosphere, of the location where convicts first formed a community in New South Wales.

Settler society in colonial Australia

White settlement in Australia was relatively small in the first three decades after the arrival of the First Fleet because the demands of the Napoleonic Wars retarded transportation. By 1810, the white population of New South Wales amounted to 12,000 convicts, military and naval personnel, and a sprinkling of free settlers such as lawyers, clergymen, and doctors. Over the next seven decades, Australia's non-Indigenous population increased substantially to reach 406,000 in 1850, on the eve of the gold rush; it then rose to 1,648,000 in 1870. The next three decades witnessed further demographic growth. Natural increase was marked throughout the century, while migration surged in the 1850s and 1880s. At the time of Federation in 1901, when Australia became a nation, the population totalled 3,770,000. Some 78% had been born in Australia; 18% in the British Isles; 2% in another European country; and less than 2% in Asian or Pacific countries.

Between 1831 and 1900, half of the 1.47 million migrants to the Australian colonies had passages subsidized by the British government. In many cases, they were recruited under the systematic colonization policies of Edward Gibbon Wakefield, whereby revenues from Australian land sales were used to subsidize passages on government-sponsored ships. But other schemes also existed whereby immigrants were selected and recruited. The great majority of settlers in Australia came from British or Irish backgrounds. For shorthand purposes, it is helpful to refer to them as Anglo-Celtic because Britain and Ireland were politically joined as part of the United Kingdom. Yet there were notable differences between the British and Irish immigrants in their religious allegiances. Most Irish immigrants were Catholic, many English settlers were Anglican, and many Scots were Presbyterian, with widely divergent views about education, culture, and politics. So 19th-century Australia was multicultural but within an Anglo-Celtic context.

Colonists came partly from middle-class professional backgrounds, but predominantly from lower-class skilled and semi-skilled occupations. Few aristocrats emigrated to Australia as they had no need to seek out opportunities in such a faraway destination. The social structure of colonial Australia was therefore heavily biased towards the bottom part of a vertical pyramid denoting social class. Apart from the predominant British and Irish contingent, other, smaller groups were found. German Lutherans helped to settle parts of South Australia in the

1830s and 1840s. Chinese migrants were found in the gold rush settlements. Polynesians and Melanesians, and a sprinkling of Italians, found work and homes in the sugar-producing, tropical zone of north Queensland. These migrants retained their ethnic identities while adapting to life in Australia. Before the 1880s, the colonists thought of themselves as Queenslanders, Victorians, South Australians, and so on; but thereafter, the white population began to view itself more self-consciously as Australians.

The growth of white settlement in Australia stemmed from various factors. Children of pioneers and ex-convicts spread beyond the Blue Mountains overland. They made homes in fertile bush areas, suitable for sheep grazing, in the interior of New South Wales and the Port Phillip District (including Australia Felix, the name supplied by Thomas Mitchell for lush pastures in western Victoria). By 1803, settlers from New South Wales also migrated to Van Diemen's Land, which became a colony in 1824. New colonies were established in Western Australia, originally known as the Swan River colony (1829), South Australia (1836), Victoria (1850), and Queensland (1859). Victoria comprised the post-1843 boundaries of the Port Phillip District. South Australia, Victoria, and Queensland were carved out of a 'greater' New South Wales. Van Diemen's Land was renamed Tasmania in 1856. Each colony established a capital city and port – Sydney in New South Wales, Hobart in Van Diemen's Land, Perth (the capital city) and Fremantle (the port) in Western Australia, Adelaide and Port Adelaide in South Australia, Melbourne in Victoria, and Brisbane in Queensland. These colonial capitals absorbed most settlers; they were connected to productive hinterlands, though less so in the case of Perth than the others. Population growth and the spread of settlement were also stimulated by economic opportunities in urban trades, pastoral occupations, and mineral excavation.

Settlers competed with Aborigines for control over land and resources. These completely different cultural groups often cooperated, but there are many examples of friction and violence. Clashes occurred between Aborigines and settlers in the Hawkesbury River area of New South Wales in the 1790s. Settlers fired upon Indigenous people, claiming they damaged their crops, and Aborigines retaliated by forming raiding parties. Between 1824 and 1836, Governor George Arthur in Van Diemen's Land was persuaded by settlers that Aborigines were a treacherous race, and so he pursued a draconian policy of driving Indigenous people away from settled areas to western fringes of the island. In 1838, the Liverpool plains area of what is now northern New South Wales experienced a series of massacres of Indigenous people, notably at Myall Creek station where, on 10 June, settlers killed 30 unarmed Aborigines as revenge for attacks on their livestock.

Contentious debate has characterized recent attempts to evaluate these frontier clashes. Evidence has surfaced about exaggerated numbers of Aboriginal deaths in resisting settlers. Determining accurate numbers of those killed is difficult, sometimes impossible, to establish, but there is little doubt of serious violence by both Aborigines and settlers. Suggestions that British and Irish settlers pursued genocidal policies are unproven, yet the savagery and loss of life in frontier areas was common. Whatever the actual numbers killed, the fact remains that Aborigines were subjugated to European settler hegemony. Aboriginal numbers suffered dramatically through violence and the spread of disease from contact with Europeans. Smallpox, for example, killed half of the Indigenous people in the Sydney Cove area in the 1790s. Settler actions and disease reduced the number of Aborigines in Van Diemen's Land from 4,000–6,000 in 1788 to 300 by the 1830s.

While Aborigines suffered from colonial expansion, settlers generally flourished. By the second half of the 19th century, Australia had acquired a reputation as a working man's paradise. Most people had better living standards than those in an equivalent position on the social scale in Britain. Australians had greater meat consumption than Britons; they earned higher wages on average; they often had better housing stock as the major cities suburbanized; they needed less winter fuel than Europeans; and workplace arrangements were protected by stronger trade unions than in Britain. By the 1880s, Manly, on Sydney's north shore, epitomized the working person's arcadia in the southern hemisphere – as the slogan put it, it was 'seven miles from Sydney and a thousand miles from care'.

This rosy picture, however, is not the whole story. Colonial Australia was more of a working man's paradise for skilled people than for the unskilled. Economic booms and busts affected employment opportunities, especially in the agricultural downturn of the early 1840s and general economic depression in the early 1890s. The highly seasonal nature of the Australian colonial workforce had important implications for working life, such as uneven earnings across one year for many workers. Moreover, there were always Australians who were out of luck and dependent on charity. Poor sanitary conditions in late 19th-century slums in Sydney and Melbourne also militated against the image of Australia as a destination for the working class to flourish.

A white bastion in the Pacific

When the Commonwealth of Australia was inaugurated in 1901, the new nation was a white bastion in the Pacific. In the debates preceding Federation, Edmund Barton, who became Australia's first prime minister, spoke about the need to preserve Australia's white Anglo-Celtic heritage and to exclude Asians from the nation: 'The doctrine of the equality of man was never intended to apply to the equality of the Englishman and the Chinaman.' Alfred Deakin, Australia's first attorney-general and thrice prime minister, echoed this sentiment. 'Australia proposes to tolerate nothing within its dominion that is not British in character and constitution or capable of becoming Anglicized without delay', he wrote. For those who could not meet these criteria because of their race, 'the policy is that of the closed door'. Two of the first acts of the Commonwealth Parliament followed through this 'White Australia Policy' – as it was unofficially known – quickly and comprehensively. The Immigration Restriction Act (1901) effectively excluded non-Europeans as migrants to Australia. The Pacific Island Labourers' Act (1902) stipulated that Polynesians, Melanesians and other islander groups should be repatriated to their home countries, and excluded emigration to Australia by such people after 1904. The formal method of exclusion was a 50-word dictation test first used in the British South African colony of Natal in 1897. A language could be selected for Asian and other non-English-speaking immigrants in such a way that it was virtually impossible for the person to pass the test.

White Australians had already discriminated against Aborigines on racial grounds since the beginning of European settlement in New South Wales. Asian immigrants posed another type of racial and cultural threat. The presence of Oriental diggers at the gold rushes had induced colonies worried by the spread of alien habits and work competition ('the yellow peril') to enact laws against the Chinese – seen as the major Asian threat to Australia – in the 1850s and early 1860s. After the gold rush era, the legislation was repealed. Friction with Chinese immigrants revived in the 1880s when they again began to arrive. By that time, cheap labour supplied by 'Kanaka' Pacific islanders in the Queensland sugar industry also stirred up racial feeling. Dissemination of Social Darwinist ideas, discriminating against Asians on racial grounds, added to the dislike of non-white settlers in Australia. Racism lay at the heart of the 'White Australia Policy' as it did in a number of other countries – South Africa and the United States among them – which aimed to restrict immigrants according to a 'global colour line' in the early 20th century.

The 'long, slow death' of white Australia meant, however, that Australia stayed largely connected to its British and Irish roots until the middle of the 20th century.

In 1958, a Migration Act abolished the dictation test and avoided reference to immigration restriction on racial grounds, but the 'White Australia Policy' continued. By that time, Australia had become a more welcoming country for immigrants from diverse cultural and geographical backgrounds, and the more positive disposition by the government towards such immigrants influenced policies towards Indigenous people. In 1966, the Australian government eased restrictions on non-European immigrants. The 'White Australia Policy' was finally dismantled in 1973: race was removed as a factor in Australia's immigration policies and immigrants could obtain citizenship after three years' residence.

The Aborigines and their struggle

Relations between white Australians and Aborigines were fraught with tension as two antithetical cultures clashed over land resources, social organization, and racial norms. Settlers considered they had the right to acquire land resources from the Indigenous owners of the soil – a practice that occurred in many other settler societies in the 19th century such as the United States, South Africa, and New Zealand. This land grabbing inevitably led to frontier violence. Punitive expeditions and violent clashes between Aborigines and settlers occurred in South Australia at Coorong lagoon in 1840, at Rufus River in 1841, and elsewhere. Other confrontations between Aborigines and settlers have already been noted. Native police forces were formed to protect frontier areas, and these sometimes resulted in Indigenous people recruited by the police force using physical force against fellow Aboriginal protesters. This was a frequent occurrence on the Queensland frontier in the 1870s. Aborigines offered stiff resistance, but settlers always held the whip hand in terms of enforcing law and order. In 1859, some Aboriginal groups in Victoria's Goulburn Valley petitioned for the return of their land and the Victorian government reserved some land for them. Similar attempts to reclaim land by Indigenous people occurred elsewhere in Australia, but rarely with positive results.

The social organization and behaviour of Aboriginal groups cut little ice with many colonial and state administrators. Officials assumed that Aborigines had little part to play in Australia's expansive development, and that they should either be cordoned off into reservations or assimilated into the white population. This reflected notions about the superiority of the white race over Indigenous people, and of the higher place accorded to grafting European civilization in the Antipodes over the customs of a backward, static race. 'The barbarous races will melt from the path of the Caucasian', the *Deniliquin Chronicle* noted on 17 February 1866, 'not by a bloody or brutal series of massacres and poisonings but by a gradual and beneficial mingling and absorption'. Separation, however, was more common than racial mixture. One notorious feature of separating the races was to take away Aboriginal children from their families. From 1883 to 1969, the New South Wales government had the right to seize such children under child welfare legislation. In the Northern Territory in the 1920s, police separated people of mixed Aboriginal and European descent from their parents. In various states, reserves were set up for darker-skinned Indigenous people, on the basis that their skin colour destined them to live apart from the rest of the Australian population. Thus, during the first half of the 20th century, Queensland Aborigines were rounded up and herded into large-scale, state-controlled reserves. The view was frequently held that the Aboriginal problem would eventually disappear as Indigenous people died rapidly from illnesses introduced by Europeans to Australia, such as gastric complaints and influenza.

Aborigines generally resisted assimilation into white Australian ways of life. Governor Lachlan Macquarie's attempts to train them as yeomen farmers in the 1810s failed because of the indifferent attitudes of Indigenous people to agricultural cultivation. Christian missionary attempts to civilize Aborigines and to acquaint them with white standards of dress, deportment, religion, and imperial loyalty were similarly unsuccessful. Greater success with intermingling Indigenous and white people was achieved in the Northern Territory and Queensland's cattle country in the early 20th century where Aborigines adjusted to settler ways of herding cattle and learned stock-work skills, which they could then adapt to their own needs. But adaptation was less frequent than either complete separation on reserves or attempts at assimilation. In the 1950s, the Commonwealth government embarked on a more thoroughgoing assimilation policy to incorporate Aborigines into Western-style education, training, and health, but this continued the separation of families. Of course, personal liaisons between white men and Aboriginal women – more common than connections between Indigenous men and white women – could be found throughout Australia by the mid-20th century, but such households often carried a social stigma.

Multicultural Australia

Since the Second World War, Australia has become a more multicultural society, both in terms of the composition of its population and its partial absorption of Indigenous people into the broader polity. The great white walls of an immigration policy largely restricted to Anglo-Celts began to be dismantled shortly after the ending of hostilities in 1945. Australia had plenty of employment opportunities for post-war economic reconstruction but experienced internal labour shortages. There was also a general view that the racial horrors of the Second World War should lead to a greater connection between ethnic, linguistic, and racial groups in the post-war world. Believing that a substantial population was needed for Australia's future, the Commonwealth government allowed thousands of Germans,

Italians, Greeks, and other Europeans to live in Australia under a massive immigration programme. By 1950, 200,000 migrants had arrived in Australia as part of this boom, many of them with government-assisted passages.

Some European migrants were refugees and displaced persons; many wished to escape poverty and unemployment; all were looking for better opportunities and more secure living standards. By the 1950s, Melbourne had inner-city areas with Greek and Italian communities, a pattern replicated in other Australian cities. British emigrants continued to settle in the thousands in Australia, many of them aided by the British government as 'ten-pound Poms' (that is, with a cheap assisted fare to emigrate). There was also considerable migration across the Tasman Sea from New Zealand. But the most recent waves of Australian immigrants have been dominated by Asians coming from China, Vietnam, Malaysia, India, Indonesia, and the Philippines. Levels of migration from parts of the Middle East to Australia have also increased. This multicultural influx has altered the composition of the Australian population. The census of 2006 reported that almost one-quarter of people living in Australia had been born elsewhere: 1.15 million were born in the United Kingdom, 477,000 in New Zealand, 220,000 in Italy, 203,000 in the People's Republic of China, 180,000 in Vietnam, 154,000 in India, 136,000 in the Philippines, and 126,000 in Greece.

Aboriginals and Torres Strait Islanders, living on hundreds of small islands in Torres Strait, which are mostly part of Queensland, now comprise 550,000 people (2.7% of the Australian population). A 1967 referendum resulted in the Commonwealth government being allowed to make laws for Aboriginal people. Power over Aboriginal affairs is shared today by the state/territory and federal governments. The first Aboriginal representative to sit in the Commonwealth of Australia's Parliament was Neville Bonner in 1971. Indigenous Australians have continued to press their claims for the restoration of land. The Mabo decision in the High Court of Australia in 1992 overturned the doctrine of *terra nullius* (i.e. no man's land) and gave Indigenous people greater rights in negotiations over land titles. In February 2008, Prime Minister Kevin Rudd issued a public apology by the Australian government for the 'stolen generations'.

Multiculturalism is not a painless process. Asian immigration to Australia has been contentious since the 1980s. More recently, Islamic Australians have been involved in controversy. Riots occurred between mainly white Australians and Lebanese Muslims – many of them Australian-born or Australian citizens – on Sydney's Cronulla beach in December 2005. In addition, Australia's decision to detain asylum-seekers – mainly from Asia – in offshore detention centres has attracted criticism from human rights supporters. Amnesty International, for instance, has attacked the detention of asylum-seekers in tents and the treatment of lone children at Christmas Island, an Australian immigrant depot in the Indian Ocean.

Multiculturalism is also problematic for Indigenous Australians. Aborigines are still often typecast as social misfits easily lured by alcohol, drifting into crime, sanctioning sexual abuse in their communities, and refusing to cooperate with white Australians. In June 2007, the federal government intervened in over 60 Indigenous communities in the Northern Territory to investigate child abuse in those communities. Yet it failed to deal in depth effectively with poor Indigenous mental health issues and the prevalence of ear, nose, and throat complaints. Dealing with the problems posed by an increasingly multicultural society is a continuing quest in Australia. Multiculturalism needs to be more fully accepted and embedded throughout Australian society, however, before it can provide a firm basis for Australia's future destiny. Many Aboriginal people resist the notion of multiculturalism because they resent being considered just one ethnic group among many in Australian society.

Chapter 2
Shaping the continent

Aborigines had cultivated land and food resources for over 50,000 years before Europeans arrived without any impulse to connect the continent's resources to a wider world. The Europeanization of Australia, however, involved more extensive exploitation of the interior for minerals and pastoralism and greater connections between Australia and distant nations through international shipping, trade, and migration. Unexpected factors helped to shape a distinctive Australian continental experience, such as the sudden discovery of gold in the early 1850s and the subsequent rush of people to the goldfields in search of their fortunes. Land availability, assisted migration, and the rise of a skilled workforce led to the growth of an expanding pastoral frontier in which bush life became embedded in Australian folk memory. Urbanization also became a prime element of the Australian experience as colonial capital cities became the magnet for the population. The growth of seaport cities as intermediaries for the exchange of Australia's raw materials for the manufactured exports of the Old World maintained strong connections between Australia and the wider world. Settler expansion into the continent's interior changed the Australian environment through human intervention. Many changes that shaped Australian cities, the bush, and the ports involved tensions between the impulse to extract natural resources, on the one hand, to facilitate economic growth and better living standards, and a respect, on the other hand, for the land and its wildlife, fauna, and flora, though historically conservation began quite late. While these changes occurred, Indigenous people adapted their livelihoods to cope, with difficulty, with the European appropriation of land aimed at 'replenishing the earth'.

The Aboriginal economy

Aborigines survived for centuries in Australia through distinctive approaches to gathering foodstuffs combined with a spiritual connection with the land. They had intimate knowledge of particular territories associated with tribal beliefs and ancestors. The rocks, bush, rivers, flora, and fauna of the landscape were the spiritual home of their ancestors, and as such they commanded respect. Aborigines had no desire for individual acquisitiveness in their material life: all food and artefacts were shared among the group in a spirit of mutuality that satisfied communal needs. Sharing provided reciprocal help in times of dearth. Aborigines had no need to acquire land through the capitalist practices, legal procedures, and expansionist mentality of white settlers; such ways of owning and exploiting the land were alien to them. Thus, there were relatively few examples of Aborigines raiding the territorial lands of other tribes. The Indigenous approach to the land and its resources was based on collective memory of specific areas and on unspoken but accepted methods of subsistence husbandry. Aborigines had no impulse towards settled agriculture in terms of cereal cultivation, since the capacity to roam their territories was an essential part of their nomadic lifestyle. Identity with the land was both an intellectual and economic feature of Aboriginal life. Indigenous people connected their whole lives, not just their food gathering, to the prophecies of their 'Dreaming' stories, which explained how the world had evolved and how they should conduct their social and personal behaviour.

Aborigines adjusted to different ecological conditions in Australia such as tropical northern forests and the dry interior, and to changes over time in climate, the habitats of food plants, game animals, and rock holes. They improved tools such as the digging stick and spatula, fishing nets, boomerangs, and woomera, and adjusted the use of hammers and spears. Their hunter-gather lifestyle did not remain static, but altered according to changed ecological and climatic conditions. In these various ways, they altered the landscape to suit their lifestyle. These patterns of Aboriginal use of land continued after white settlement, but Indigenous groups adapted to the colonizers' expansionism and land acquisition. Aboriginal work was important for sheep farmers in Western Australia and central Queensland, and for domestic labour in inland towns and mining camps in northern and central Australia. Around 10,000 Aborigines were working for Europeans in 1900. Aborigines adapted to the animals introduced by white men to Australia, devising new techniques to trap and spear cattle and sheep and building larger ovens than previously to cook meat. They also helped European explorers with their skilled bushcraft to find water and food on expeditions.

Girt by sea

The Australian National Anthem proclaims that 'our home is girt (i.e. surrounded) by sea', a reminder of the important maritime dimension to life down under. In the centuries before white settlement, northern Australia had maritime connections with the Macassan trepang fishery for the Chinese market and boats from Java and other parts of Indonesia occasionally touched at Australian shores. The Aboriginal population mainly concentrated on land resources, though small craft were used for fishing or local transport. Australia's maritime development came gradually with European settlement. Its beginnings can be traced back to 1788 with the settling of a convict colony, with naval ships and officers, at Port Jackson. Since then, Australian life has been crucially influenced by the interaction between its people and the sea. The access to ports by all the state capital cities, the growth of shipping and ship-owning, the progress of coastal, regional, and overseas trade, the development of merchant firms, and links between the major port gateways and their hinterlands have all shaped the modern Australian economy. The emergence of a strong maritime workforce has been part of radical trade unionism in the southern hemisphere. The growth of tourism, beach culture, ferries, and harbour services have also been essential features of modern Australian social history and leisure.

Each Australian state capital is located on or near a port site, giving access to the ocean and linking the shore with productive hinterlands. This reflects the white settlement of Australia, which was initially based on communities within easy reach of the coast. Sydney and Hobart, both with fine natural harbours, were flourishing centres for shipping and trade by the early 19th century. In both cases, wharves and quays were the site of the first houses in each city, and the pattern of housing stretched inland from these initial sites. Adelaide and Melbourne had locations respectively on the Torrens and Yarra rivers, with ports eventually built at Port Adelaide and Port Melbourne. Williamstown also served as a port for Melbourne. Brisbane had a riverside setting. Perth, on the Swan River, had no suitable harbour for vessels, owing to the shallowness of the estuary on which it is situated. Therefore Fremantle, which had suitable depth of water, was built as the main port to service Perth and its hinterland. Each of these cities established shipping facilities and gradually became linked in coastal and regional trade. Overseas liners worked around the coast to discharge the goods they brought and take on cargo for the return voyage. In the coastal trade, the Australasian Steam Navigation Company – one of a number of national companies – played a leading role in the coastal trade between the 1850s and 1880s, with ships able to sail between Rockhampton in Queensland around the continent to Albany in Western Australia.

Britain dominated long-distance shipping to Australia in the 19th century. The relaxation of the English East India Company's charter in 1813 gave its vessels more incentive to come to Australia because of the lure of cargoes. But passengers became equally as important as freight in stimulating shipping services as convicts were sent on naval vessels to New South Wales before 1840 and free emigrants took up government assisted passages. Steam services between Europe and Australia, which began regularly in 1852, were dominated by British-owned vessels. Isambard Kingdom Brunel's *SS Great Britain* became a notable passenger vessel on the London–Melbourne run by the 1850s. By 1860, the Peninsular & Oriental Steam Company (P&O) dominated long-distance passenger business to Australia. Liner shipping conferences and agreements between steamship companies in Australian overseas trade existed from the 1880s, mainly under British control. Mergers and combinations of shipping companies over the next few decades usually favoured British rather than Australian investors. By the end of the First World War, Lord Inchcape's leadership of merged companies, including P&O, gave Britain unrivalled power over Australian coastal, regional, and intercontinental trades.

After the Second World War, major changes occurred in Australia's deployment of shipping. Vessels flourished under Australian ownership, especially the large ships carrying bulk cargoes of mineral resources and tankers carrying crude oil for large corporations. The major Australian-owned company in the coastal trade was the Australian National Line. By the 1970s, containerization had become an important part of Australia's shipping industry, with roll-on, roll-off cargoes revolutionizing the landscape of ports. By 1997, the largest carriers could lift over 6,000 containers with about 70,000 tonnes of freight. The growth of jet travel by air led to the decline of passenger liners, but they were often redeployed into the mass business of cruising at sea. Specialized vessels, including refrigerated fruit carriers and car carriers, have also proliferated at Australian ports since the 1970s.

External commerce has drawn Australia into a wider trading world that is essential for the economic livelihood of its citizens.

The remoteness of the first European settlements made long-distance trade problematic: ships could take the best part of a year to sail from Sydney to London. This 'tyranny of distance' was eventually overcome in the mid-19th century by steam navigation and communications improvements made possible by the electric cable telegraph. But the vast distance from Europe made it imperative that Australians find suitable products to ship to Europe in exchange for the manufactured products of Britain's Industrial Revolution. This entailed the search for staple exports. Before the 1820s, whaling and sealing were flourishing maritime trades in Australian waters, but both trades had declined permanently by the 1840s. The rapid growth of the pastoral frontier in New South Wales and Australia Felix between 1820 and 1850 led to a surge in wool exports, which comprised over two-thirds of colonial Australia's total export income by 1850. Wool remained the leading export from Australia to the mother country for generations apart from gold, which surpassed it after 1851 for two decades. Wool benefited from the fact that the wool press could reduce the weight of wool carried on board vessels by three-quarters. The gold rush of the 1850s produced an important mineral for export. Australian ships also exported wheat and, from the 1880s, refrigerated meat and dairy products to Britain. Coal was also exported from Australia, but it was not until the late 1930s that bulk carriers were built in Australia to carry coal overseas. Australia's industrialization enabled a 'seaport industrial machine' to integrate raw materials and metallurgical industry onto bulk carriers by the 1960s.

Australian trade with the wider world was not confined to long-distance connections with Britain. Sandalwood was exported in the 19th century to China. Tahitian pork was imported for consumption in Australian homes. Tea, sugar, and rice were commodities that linked Asia with Australia. On the eve of the First World War, France bought more than half of Australia's wool and hides, and Belgium and Germany took most of the zinc and almost half of the copper. Nevertheless, Anglo-Australian commodity trade was still dominant, with 60% of Australia's import income coming from the United Kingdom, and 44% of Australia's exports by value being sent to the UK in 1913. It was only after the Second World War that Anglo-Australian trade gradually declined as a share of total Australian commodity trade. By 1966–8, the UK provided 22% of Australia's imports and took 13% of Australia's exports by value: Australia now imported more goods from the United States than from Britain and one-third of Australia's exports were dispatched to Japan and other Asian markets. These trade trends accelerated after the UK joined the European Economic Community in 1973 and began to whittle down significant components of its traditional trade with Australia (especially in refrigerated meat). Asian markets rapidly began to take a larger share of Australia's foreign trade: Asia now accounts by value for over three-quarters of Australia's exports and for around half of Australia's imports. The People's Republic of China overtook Japan to become Australia's largest trading partner in 2009.

The impact of the bush

Urban and rural Australia both flourished in the 19th century, though in the popular imagination Australia was associated more with the 'bush' than with cities. Life in the bush was associated particularly with the itinerant workers who toiled in lonely locations, moving from place to place in search of work. They were predominantly male, and mainly comprised employees in the pastoral industry: semi-nomadic drovers, shepherds, shearers, bullock-drivers, stockmen, and overlanders. G. C. Mundy succinctly characterized the typical bushman as 'tall and spare, wiry and active, with face, hands, and throat burnt to a ruddy bronze, his saddle seemed his natural home'. Helping one another to endure tough lives, such men contributed to the 'bush legend' as an integral part of Australia's identity. They became renowned for their independence, resourcefulness, hardy natures, and stoicism, cultivating 'mateship' among their co-workers. Russel

Ward's *The Australian Legend* (1958) claimed a central place for this rural proletariat in the making of modern Australia, arguing that their toughness, egalitarianism, endurance, and masculine conviviality stemmed from the convict era. These same qualities informed the 'diggers' in the two World Wars. Ballads and popular songs by Henry Lawson and A. B. 'Banjo' Paterson depicted the lives of the bushmen. Australian painters celebrated bush life with pictures of shearers at work in golden light. These writers and painters, however, were usually based in the large Australian cities. Their creative work is as much a case of urban nostalgia for an imagined existence in the bush as an accurate portrayal of rural life in Australia.

There was an underside to life in the Australian bush. Rural areas were frequently the site of conflict between several groups: squatters and small-scale agriculturalists, Crown land agents and people eking out a living on small homesteads, a downtrodden rural proletariat and the police. Squatters had occupied undeveloped land since the 1820s, mainly living on the profits of tending sheep and cattle. Their access to land was challenged in the 1860s when the colonial governments introduced legislation that allowed 'selectors' to acquire land at a minimal price. The intention of these Land Acts was to promote homesteads based on intensive agriculture, but that was rarely achieved. Those who forged an anti-establishment role in such an environment were bushrangers, found mainly in New South Wales, Victoria, and Van Diemen's Land/Tasmania between 1815 and 1880. Armed and often operating in gangs, bushrangers, also known as bolters, engaged in cattle- and horse-stealing; they attacked the property of harsh taskmasters; and they never wittingly preyed upon the rural poor. They created an image of lawlessness in outback Australia, behaving as self-appointed righters of wrongs to some but as threats to private property by others. Ward argued that bushrangers had considerable appeal to Australians because of their bravery and independence.

The most famous bushranger was Ned Kelly, the son of a former convict from Irish stock. Kelly grew up on an impoverished farm in northeast Victoria, and had an engrained hatred for the big squatters, supported by the law, the courts, and the police, in curtailing the land rights of small farmers. Kelly became a bushranger in the 1870s after serving several prison sentences for assault and robbery. He and his gang stole horses, robbed banks, shot policemen, and spent two years on the run. They were cornered at Glenrowan, Victoria, in 1880. Three of the gang were killed. Ned Kelly was captured, wearing bullet-proof armour he had made from the mullboards of farmers' ploughs. He was tried,

3. Ned Kelly, Australian bushranger

sentenced to death, and hanged in Melbourne on 11 November 1880. After having robbed a bank in the southern New South Wales town of Jerilderie, Kelly produced an 8,300-word testament called the 'Jerilderie letter', stating his grievances and political views. This rambling document shows Kelly's sympathy for the downtrodden rural poor and his accusations of bad practice by the police: he hoped money could be given

> to the widows and orphans and poor of Greta district where I spent and will again spend many a happy day fearless free and bold as it only aids the police to procure false witnesses and go whacks with men to steal horses and lag innocent men it would suit them far better to subscribe a sum and give it to the poor of their district.

The gold rush

Gold was discovered by chance in New South Wales in February 1851, followed by further, larger finds of alluvial deposits in Victoria later in the same year. The discovery of these nuggets of gold created an instant reaction. This supply-side shock to the economy dominated the 1850s in the Antipodes. Just as in California in 1849, the gold rush in Australia saw people from all walks of life and many occupations flock to the gold fields in search of their fortunes. Gold prospectors also sailed from around the globe to Melbourne to join the quest for riches; they came from Britain, Continental Europe, China, and the United States. Nationalities jostled together in gold-mining areas. Many on the gold fields had been Chartists, or among the Continental Europeans caught up in the 1848 revolutions. 'This very large society', a Polish miner recalled of the levelling experience on the goldfields,

> comprises men from all parts of the world, all countries and religions, varying dispositions and education ... all mixed into one society, all dressed similarly ... Here we are all joined by a common designation: digger.

In such an atmosphere of excitement, greed, and individualism, egalitarianism was none the less promoted. 'All the aristocratic feelings and associations of the old country', wrote an observer at the gold rush in 1853, were,

> at once annihilated.... It is not what you were, but what you are, that is the criterion... by which you are judged; and although your father might have been my Lord of England-all-over, it goes for nothing in this equalizing colony of gold and beef and mutton.

Diggers at the gold rushes had diverse experiences. In 1852, 35,000 prospectors extracted more than £16 million of gold; but in 1854, 100,000 miners produced just over half that sum. As the 1850s progressed, finding new precious lodes became ever more difficult, and the gold rush was over by 1860. For every miner who struck lucky in finding gold, thousands more ended up empty-handed, though deep mining remained important in Victoria for a further couple of decades. Later rushes to be rich occurred in New South Wales, Queensland, and finally in Western Australia, where gold was discovered in the 1890s. But never again did gold discoveries have such a major impact on Australia. While they lasted, however, they boosted colonial Australia's population and economy. Victoria's population, stimulated mainly by the prospect of gold and the services it required, grew rapidly from around 100,000 in 1851 to 540,000 a decade later. New South Wales's population rose less rapidly in this decade, but still increased from c. 200,000 to 350,000. Gold stimulated housing and the retail trades in those two colonies. It boosted the development of Melbourne. It also attracted British investment capital from mining companies and British shipping companies' services to transport miners from overseas to the diggings.

Tensions arose, however, on the gold fields in Victoria and New South Wales. Licences were required to dig for gold. On Crown land, they were initially 30 shillings per month, which lay beyond the means of most miners. Labourers could claim a mining plot of

4. Cradling and panning for gold in an Australian mine

12 feet square in Victoria. Disputes arose over access to land, the payment for licences, and the heavy-handed police (often ex-convicts) who patrolled the gold fields. The barricading of diggers at the Eureka stockade, outside Ballarat, in December 1854, was a symbolic stand of miners against the forces of authority. It led to a 20-minute skirmish between miners and the police, resulting in the deaths of over 30 diggers and 4 soldiers; 130 protesters were taken prisoner. Though exaggerated as a landmark in Australia's developing political consciousness, the incident led to a miner's right of £1 per year replacing the detested licences.

The other main tensions present on the gold fields involved racial hostility between miners and the Chinese – the chief overseas group of non-Anglo-Celtic stock who panned for gold. The Chinese were regarded as heathen, dirty, non-Christian, opium-smokers, and stigmatized as the 'yellow peril'. A colonist claimed the Chinese were 'constantly exposed to insult and annoyance' and 'ruthlessly driven from their claims as soon as their wash-dirt showed any symptoms of richness'. Victoria, New South Wales, and South Australia all passed discriminatory laws against the entry of Chinese migrants, but these were repealed after the gold fever died down. An anti-Chinese riot occurred at Lambing Flat, New South Wales, in July 1861, in which 6,000 diggers turned on the Chinese. Police, soldiers, and sailors were drafted to quell the disturbance. Graves of Chinese miners in cemeteries in Victoria are a reminder of the Chinese influx at the gold rush of the 1850s.

Land settlement

The post-gold-rush era precipitated land hunger. Many Australians wanted to purchase land to make a living. Selection Acts passed by the Australian colonies in the 1860s and 1870s enabled them to do so. The relevant laws involved surveying the Crown land leased to squatters and the sale of lots up to 640 acres at an affordable price. Purchasers were required to fence the land, build a house, and cultivate one acre in ten. From the 1880s onwards, some colonies turned to closer settlement as a further experiment in resettling the land. Under this scheme, only land suitable for agriculture with access to markets was available. Another initiative in land settlement came after the end of the First World War when the Commonwealth and state governments devised soldier settlement schemes to encourage veterans to seek their livelihoods in rural Australia.

All these initiatives were concerned with promoting Australia's demographic growth and use of land and agricultural resources. They were aimed at immigrants as much as Australians. The schemes had varied results. Much of Australia's soil remained unsuited to settled agriculture; selectors (i.e. small farmers) often had insufficient capital and inadequate agricultural knowledge and skills; land was often transferred back to squatters; and returned soldiers invariably had problems of adjustment to a new civilian life in lonely rural areas. Despite these problems, there was a high rate of success in the Riverina, western Victoria, and later Western Australia; cereal production increased substantially and the family farm became the unit of rural enterprise.

The efforts of settlers on the land have contributed to the Pioneer Legend as a potent symbol of Australian development. Pioneers included stockmen, itinerant workers, squatters, and small farmers. They often lived with their families in challenging rural conditions. They battled to carve out a living from the land, hoping to hand on the fruits of their property and capital from one generation to the next. They displayed hard work, enterprise, courage, and toughness. This view of Australia's settlement places less emphasis on class division than the Bush Legend, and points to an enduring Anglo-Celtic culture in rural settlements. It is profoundly at odds with the multiethnic and multicultural composition of people today in Australia's state capital cities. But the Pioneer Legend created an Australian identity to the settlers and immigrants who had overcome the hardships of settlement on the sheep-runs, cattle stations, and outback farms. Sometimes staving off Aboriginal attacks was part of taming the land.

City life

Despite the potency of the Bush Legend, most Australian settlers in the 19th century were attracted to city life. By the time of Federation, 40% of Victoria's population lived in Melbourne; 37% of people in New South Wales were based in Sydney; 39% of South Australia's population lived in Adelaide; 38% of Western Australians resided in Perth; 23% of Queenslanders were located in Brisbane; and 21% of Tasmanians lived in Hobart. By 1900, Australia was a more urbanized society than other countries of recent settlement such as Argentina, New Zealand, Canada, and the United States. Australian urbanization has increased significantly since Federation. Figures for 2006 show that 63% of people in New South Wales lived in Sydney; 71% of people in

Victoria have homes in Melbourne; 46% of Queensland's population resides in Brisbane; 74% of South Australians live in Adelaide; 75% of West Australians live in Perth; and 41% of Tasmanians are located in Hobart.

Colonial (later state) capital cities were originally commercial centres created by settlers. All were based within reach of rivers and the ocean. They developed harbours and docks to facilitate maritime shipping and trade; served as conduits for the exchange of manufactured imported goods for Australia's agricultural produce and mineral resources; and were also seats of government and providers of services. These cities lacked an established upper class. Though they had poor areas, such as Redfern in Sydney and Collingwood in Melbourne, each city had a sizeable retail sector and middle-class professionals. Australian cities copied the suburban ideals found in Britain's Victorian cities. Suburbs with house after house, connected by efficient transport services to the places of employment, became the norm, with workers attracted to the cities by generally good wages. An emigrant from Birmingham in Britain to Sydney towards the end of Queen Victoria's reign would have experienced different climatic conditions but little real difference in the layout and amenities of city life. In 1898, Sidney and Beatrice Webb wrote that 'Society in Australia...is just a slice of Great Britain and differs only slightly from Glasgow, Manchester, Liverpool and the suburbs of London.'

By the time Australia became a nation, it was widely agreed that her main cities provided pleasant urban environments and good living standards. They were

> hives of workers, with no idle classes of dilettante or mere pleasure-seekers, and with hardly a millionaire. They show what communities of busy people, seldom very rich, as seldom miserably poor, can do in the way of organizing a decent, orderly, progressive civilization.

The possibility of home-ownership for settlers of modest background was a drawing card for city life. In 1858, W. S. Jevons, a migrant from England to Sydney, wrote, with a degree of hyperbole, that

> almost every labourer and mechanic here has his own residence on freehold or leasehold land, and unpretending as it is to any convenience or beauties it yet satisfies him better than the brick-built closely-packed rented houses of English towns.

By the last quarter of the 19th century, 30–40% of the houses in Sydney and Melbourne were owner-occupied.

Two types of city characterized the Australian urban experience: high-density cities and low-density cities. The former included Sydney, Brisbane, and Hobart, all of which initially developed a crowded and unplanned city core. These were walking cities, in the European tradition, and they were congested urban spaces before 1900, largely based around inner suburbs. The urban landscape of such high-density cities was often unconducive to public transport such as tramways, streetcars, railways, and buses. Thus, Sydney's Central Station is located several miles from the harbour owing to the higgledy-piggledy layout and terrain of the city's streets. Melbourne, Adelaide, and Perth, by contrast, were lower-density cities, in which extensive suburbs stretch for miles beyond the city's inner core. These cities had more street planning on a grid pattern, and were better able to construct transport services to outer suburbs. Melbourne's tram network was, and is, the epitome of providing transport services in a low-density city. Melbourne, Adelaide, and Perth have been regarded as part of the 'new urban frontier' of the century after 1840, for their layout is similar to the pattern of urban development found in the American West and Canada in cities such as Los Angeles, Denver, and Vancouver. During the 20th century, the distinction between high- and low-density Australian cities became less obvious: the differences now are hard to discern, and Brisbane sprawls more than Melbourne or Adelaide.

Sydney and Melbourne have always vied for the place of premier Australian city. Sydney, an earlier settlement than Melbourne, was originally the larger of the two. But Melbourne's population increased dramatically during the gold rush of the 1850s to overtake Sydney. Melbourne also grew rapidly as a financial and commercial centre, attracting banks and British capital. In 1880, a large domed Royal Exhibition building displayed its growth and progress. Melbourne became known as 'Marvellous Melbourne' during the construction boom of the 1880s when its population passed half a million and it was described as 'the metropolis of the Southern Hemisphere'. Sydney's population passed Melbourne's in the early 20th century and has remained larger, with Melbourne sometimes growing faster and sometimes falling behind; they now have about 4.6 and 4.1 million people respectively. By the 1920s, in Melbourne and Sydney, as in other Australian cities, suburban housing had spread well beyond the original inner core of the city, with street after street of standardized, detached, single-storey bungalows set in quarter-acre blocks.

Both Sydney and Melbourne have distinctive cultural, social, sporting, and political traditions that militate against an attempt to categorize them as embracing an archetypal Australian metropolis. They are the only Australian cities large enough to have hosted an Olympic Games – Melbourne in 1956 and Sydney in 2000. Their rivalry was such that Canberra had to be specially created as Australia's capital city. By 1971, four out of every ten Australians lived in either Melbourne or Sydney. Perth, Adelaide, and Brisbane, which were more like large country towns than cities before the Second World War, are also now large modern metropolises, acting as service centres to the agriculture, industry, and trade of their hinterlands and each with international airports. Perth, the only major Australian city facing the Indian Ocean, has become a vibrant centre for Western Australia's resource industries; its population is now 1.6 million. Adelaide, a base for Australia's defence industries, has 1.3 million people.

Brisbane, which has the largest economy of any city between Sydney and Singapore, is home to 2 million people.

Education

Different types of schools were established in colonial Australia. Sunday schools spread widely throughout New South Wales during the governorship of Lachlan Macquarie between 1810 and 1821. They offered Christian moral instruction and help with literacy through the practice of displaying the words of hymns on lined paper. Day schools for the poor expanded in the first half of the 19th century, maintained by the government and overseen by Anglican chaplains. By the 1830s, schools run by the churches were given subsidies. The type of religious instruction in schools proved contentious, however, as much rivalry existed between Anglicans, Roman Catholics, and non-denominational groups: each wanted to spread its own version of Christianity. During the 1830s, Governor Richard Bourke of New South Wales introduced a system whereby all types of Christian instruction were allowed in schools. Rather than being under the control of the master or mistress, this was ministered once a week by the different Christian ministers visiting the school. The religious tensions in the school system continued until the 1870s and 1880s, when the Australian colonies passed Education Acts that established a centrally administered state school system based upon secular instruction. Financial aid was then removed from all denominational schools. By the time of Federation, each Australian colony had framed its own free, compulsory, and secular educational laws.

Apart from day schools for the poor mentioned above, there were bush schools in the outback, mission schools for Aborigines, schools with German-language instruction in areas of Lutheran settlement, such as South Australia's Barossa Valley, and grammar schools for secondary-age pupils. Geelong Grammar School, founded in 1857, and Sydney Grammar School, which opened in 1854, were two prominent independent schools influenced by

Thomas Arnold's Rugby School. State high schools emerged in the early 20th century. Many of them were academically selective and adopted the ethos of independent schools. Comprehensive secondary schools emerged in the 1950s and 1960s, with a mixed-ability intake to cater for most state school students. Today, most Australian children are educated in state schools funded by government. But Catholic schools, with most staff and students practising the Roman Catholic faith, and independent schools, sometimes catering for boarders, also exist.

The most common type of instruction used in 19th-century elementary schools in Australia was the monitorial system, first devised in England, in which the older, numerate, and literate children were trained as monitors to teach the younger children. This was a cheap and effective way for imparting the three Rs before the evolution of a pupil-teacher apprenticeship system, which was later replaced by more professional instruction in teacher-training colleges by the early 20th century. The curriculum followed in 19th-century Australian schools varied considerably. Geelong Grammar, for example, followed the emphasis on teaching the Classics and encouraging team sport along Arnoldian lines, while Scotch College, Melbourne, reflected its roots by emphasis upon modern languages, English literature, and science. In contemporary Australia, a national curriculum is delivered under the auspices of the Australian Curriculum, Assessment and Reporting Authority. This independent body offers a national data and assessment programme that supports learning for all Australian schoolchildren in the 21st century.

Australia has long developed adult and tertiary education. Mechanics' Institutes and free libraries, offering evening lectures, discussion groups, and access to books and newspapers for improving skilled workmen, were flourishing by the 1840s in large cities and some smaller towns. Universities came to complement and extend such intellectual endeavours for the academically able. They developed slowly: only six were founded before the First

World War, beginning with the University of Sydney in 1850 and ending with the University of Western Australia in 1911. Influenced heavily by British universities, these 'sandstone' institutions were all supported by state governments. A boost to research in the tertiary sector came with the foundation of the Australian National University in Canberra in 1946. This placed emphasis on high-quality research programmes through its various research schools. Since the 1960s, as in other Western democracies, new universities have been added to the educational landscape, including La Trobe University, on the outskirts of Melbourne, and Flinders University, in suburban Adelaide. In 2011, Australia has 39 universities.

An industrial nation

Australia's manufacturing capacity developed slowly. During the 19th century, agriculture and trade were more important sectors of the colonial Australian economy than industry. Most manufacturing was carried out in small workshops, chiefly with handicraft techniques and hand tools, and it catered mainly for the domestic market. Before Federation, most manufacturing took the form of small-scale production that focused on the processing of rural products and raw materials, assembly and repair work, and the manufacture of soap, candles, beer, and a limited amount of textile clothing. The period of the gold rush was followed by greater extractive activity of minerals such as tin and copper in South Australia, lead and silver in New South Wales and Tasmania, and coal-mining in coastal parts of New South Wales. In 1885, the establishment in western New South Wales of Broken Hill Proprietary Limited (BHP), a producer of base metals, indicated the potential for large-scale company participation in extracting mineral resources. Steel works were added at Broken Hill in 1915. Manufacturing began to grow more broadly and rapidly in Australia in the period 1901–14, spreading to cover agricultural machinery and refrigeration equipment.

Between the two World Wars of the 20th century, Australian manufacturing spread further into the growth of the steel industry, automobile assembly, and increased use of electricity. Motor vehicles on Australian roads, for instance, increased from 9,000 in 1920 to 571,000 in 1929, while large steel works grew at Newcastle, on the northern coast of New South Wales. Australia's small manufacturing buildings gave way to factories. Handicraft techniques and horsepower were replaced by machines. Mechanization was greatest in industries where labour was scarce or expensive. Thus, coal-cutting machines were developed for coalmines and shearing machines for the sheep-shearing season. The Great Depression years between 1929 and 1931 led to setbacks in industrial growth, but recovery followed as Australia's manufacturing output rose from a value of £51.3 million in 1931/2 to £79.2 million in 1938/9.

Australia produced large quantities of munitions during the Second World War. It was not until after 1945, however, that it became an advanced industrial economy with rapid manufacturing growth in automobiles, chemicals, iron and steel, electricity, and electronic equipment. Factories increased in number by 15% during the war. The growth was maintained in the 20 years after 1945 during which Australia experienced a long economic boom with full employment. The Secondary Industries Commission, formed as part of the Department of Postwar Reconstruction, oversaw the conversion of munitions factories to peacetime uses mainly for the home market. By the early 1960s, Australian manufacturers were producing millions of refrigerators, electric and gas stoves, radio and television sets, and large quantities of furniture for the home market.

In the 1950s and 1960s, minerals played a large part in Australia's industrial production: coal from New South Wales and central Queensland, iron ore from the Pilbara district of Western Australia, bauxite at Weipa in North Queensland and along the Darling Range of Western Australia, and oil off the Gippsland coast in Victoria all contributed significantly to the mineral boom. Today, minerals retain their importance for the Australian economy. BHP is Australia's largest commercial organization, operating in over 70 nations worldwide. Mining operations and the petroleum business lie at the core of its operations. Steel production was also a major part of BHP until 2002, when it was spun off to form a separate business group. But despite the high profile of a large conglomerate such as BHP (once known as 'the Big Australian'), manufacturing has experienced relative decline in recent decades as the Australian economy has become more service-based. Financial, retail, tourism, entertainment, health, education, IT, and telecommunications all play important roles in the service economy. By the start of the new millennium, services comprised 70% of Australian national income. This important sector of the economy is currently performing well. Though Australia experienced a mild recession, the global economic crisis since 2008 has been mitigated by the continuing Asian demand for Australian commodities and by the relatively low exposure of Australia's banks to sub-prime debts.

Environmentalism

The Australian environment has constantly evolved over time, partly as a result of natural factors. In the many centuries that Aborigines were the sole inhabitants of Australia, some 15% of the land surface sank below sea level, various large animals became extinct, and the continent's interior became more arid. But human factors have also had a major impact on the Australian environment over two centuries of white settlement. These have involved a thrust towards exploiting the land, a process that has only been checked partially and gradually since about the 1880s. Aborigines themselves altered the rural environment by their fire-stick techniques. These methods drove game out of scrub or bracken and favoured the growth of plant species that reproduced after exposure to fire. But Aborigines were familiar with the dryness of the Australian outback, and were well placed to balance gathering food with water preservation and available food resources.

The spread of the pastoral frontier had a major environmental impact in the 19th century. Timber resources were regularly exploited for the mining and railway industries and for domestic firewood for kitchen stoves, fireplaces, and bath heaters. Gold-mining, in particular, had a large demand for timber: the country surrounding gold-mining towns was often levelled bare, leaving no shelter from trees against wind or dust. By the late 19th century, extensive cargoes of Australian hardwoods, such as cedar and pine, were exported. Pastoralists undertook ring barking as a cheap and simple way of creating more grazing land. This destroyed the internal tissues of the trees, but it was necessary because Australia had over a 100 million sheep and nearly 8 million cattle by 1890. Sheep-runs required fencing, but extensive grazing caused soil erosion after about 20 years. The introduction of rabbits led to the disappearance of some native grasses and the stripping of bark from young saplings. Rabbits competed with sheep and cattle for grasses and reduced the extent of Australia's wool clip. Animals affected by environmental exploitation included, before 1850, the sale of kangaroo and platypus skins for the export trade, the slaughter of fur seals from Australia's south coast, and the killing of whales for whale oil. Koalas were also killed for their furs. Several types of kangaroos, wallabies, and emus were extinct by 1900. Even as late as the 1960s, thousands of kangaroos were killed to meet the demand for pet food for suburban cats and dogs; and they are still slaughtered for commercial purposes – for their meat and skin.

Australia's colonies had neither the trained personnel nor the vision to protect the land, but between the 1860s and the 1930s growing awareness of the need for new policies towards the natural and animal environment emerged. Most initiatives, undertaken at colony or state level, concerned bush areas rather than uninhabitable outback land. From the 1860s, colonial governments began to protect the coastal foreshore and the banks of lakes and streams for public use. In 1879, for instance, the New South Wales government established a 73,000-hectare area south of Sydney as a Royal National Park for the perpetual use of the public. The park soon became a popular destination for picnics and bushwalking. In 1887, the Victorian government set aside 167 hectares at Ferntree Gully as a nature reserve that became a sanctuary for lyrebirds and other wildlife. At the turn of the 20th century, state governments displayed a growing concern for irrigation and water conservation. In New South Wales, this led to the construction on the Murray River system of the Hume Reservoir between 1919 and 1931, with the Hume Dam completed in 1936, and Lake Victoria formed in 1928. The Murray-Darling basin now has salt interception schemes to pump and drain saline water flows and dispose of them by evaporation.

There were also moves towards protection of native forestry in connection with the creation of national parks. In 1906, the Queensland Parliament passed a state Forests and National Parks Act which upheld the main principles of conservation and renewal but allowed the government to establish national parks in areas without enough marketable timber to justify protection as forestry resources. In 1915, Tasmania was the first state government to pass a Scenery Preservation Act, which set up a board responsible for permanent reserves in regions of outstanding scenic merit. The Australian Conservation Foundation, a non-profit, non-governmental organization, was established in 1965. This served as a watchdog for controversial schemes relating to natural resources, such as the expansion of mining company operations. It sought to protect the Great Barrier Reef against excessive tourism, oil drilling, and the depredations of crown-of-thorns starfish. More recently, similar initiatives have been carried out at both state and federal level. The Whitlam government (1972–5) first formulated a federal conservation policy. In 1975, the Australian government established the Australian National Parks and

Wildlife Service and enacted the Great Barrier Reef Marine Park Act. In 1982, Queensland's government introduced protective legislation for the Reef. The Commonwealth exercised its powers to compel the states to comply with conservation measures, partly through export powers and later by use of its foreign affairs power as a signatory to international covenants.

Moves to protect the Australian environment became more explicitly political in the late 20th century, with the emergence of 'green' politicians, especially in Tasmania. Between 1971 and 1974, trade unions in the building industry in New South Wales helped to preserve the natural and built environment through 'green bans' – refusals to work on harmful construction projects. During the 1980s and 1990s, the 'green' movement concentrated its energies on the preservation of forest or wilderness rather than the urban environment. Particular attention was paid to the maintenance of Australia's rainforests in Tasmania and Queensland. The Aboriginal advance over land rights in the aftermath of the Mabo judgement of 1992 led to an escalation of Indigenous claims over bush areas, which were often in direct conflict with the intentions of private mining and industrial companies to exploit the land's resources. More recently, however, Aboriginal owners have favoured development against conservationists.

As Australia entered the 21st century, international concerns about climate change and global warming also influenced Australia's attitudes towards preservation of the natural environment. Severe episodes of drought and bush fires in recent years have raised alarm bells for the stability of the Australian environment. Coral bleaching on the Great Barrier Reef has started to affect the world's most diverse ocean ecosystem. The Australian government's concern to tackle greenhouse gas emissions, and thereby prevent global warming, is based on attempts to improve energy efficiency, to reduce carbon pollution, and to invest in renewable energy technologies. In August 2009, the Australian Parliament passed a measure aiming to ensure that renewable energy comprises one-fifth of electricity supply in Australia by 2020. But plans to control emissions by carbon trading were abandoned, and the current plans for a tax are based on a much smaller reduction of emissions.

Chapter 3
Governing Australia

The government of Australia has changed in scope and substance since the early days of white settlement. In 1788, New South Wales was administered by a governor, sent out from Britain, who decided all major political decisions on the spot. He was bound by instructions from the Colonial Office and his ultimate authority depended on the approval of the Imperial Parliament. Other Australian colonies followed suit by acquiring governors and, in due course, legislative councils to carry out the business of government. In the 1850s, Britain granted self-government to the Australian colonies. The colonists promptly set about establishing legislatures except for Western Australia, which did not become self-governing until 1890. The growth to maturity of Australian legislative politics, coupled with the rise of a movement towards Federation, led to the creation of a nation on 1 January 1901. The colonial parliaments continued uninterrupted, but surrendered some powers to the federal Parliament, and were now known as states rather than colonies.

Party politics proliferated in Australia during the 20th century, with Labor and various non-Labor parties dominating the political scene. Australia has become a largely peaceful medium-sized democracy, but today it is still under the constitutional aegis of the British Crown. The governor-general remains formally the representative of the British monarchy in Australia, but is now nominated by the Australian prime minister. The Union Jack is displayed on the corner of the Australian flag as a symbol of the enduring political connection between Britain and Australia. Discussions about whether Australia should become a republic have surfaced periodically and gathered momentum in the 1990s; but Australians rejected becoming a republic in a referendum held in 1999.

Colonial dependencies

The governing of Australia between the arrival of the First Fleet and the emergence of self-government in the early 1850s was largely centred on the first and largest colony, New South Wales, but also included political institutions in Van Diemen's Land, South Australia and Western Australia. In all cases, the political and legal establishment closely reflected existing British institutions. Australian colonists, whether convict or free, were entitled to legal rights according to English common law. Convicts had to serve out their criminal sentences, but thereafter they were free subjects. In political terms, the Australian colonies, as was the case in Britain, did not operate as a democracy. Before the gold rush era, settlers had limited means of exercising their political preferences through voting at elections. On a franchise restricted according to property qualifications, however, they did vote from the 1840s for a legislative council.

New South Wales was initially governed solely by a governor. Early incumbents were naval men appointed after a life of professional service under military discipline. They included the first governor, Arthur Phillip, who arrived with the First Fleet, and John Hunter, who ended up as a high-ranking naval officer. The most contentious early governor was William Bligh; the one who left the most positive mark was Lachlan Macquarie. Bligh was already controversial before he arrived in New South Wales because of his stern reputation as a naval commander that led most of his crew to turn against him in the mutiny on the *Bounty* in 1789. Bligh's term as governor ended after he challenged the New South Wales' Corps control of the government store in Sydney in the 'Rum' rebellion of 1808, which led to the only armed takeover of government (albeit temporary) in Australian history. Macquarie came from Scotland to Australia, and governed New South Wales for just over a decade until 1821. He improved public works (new towns, buildings, roads) and instructed explorers in 1813 to find a passable westward route over the Blue Mountains from Sydney to the rolling grassland beyond the hills. He attempted to 'civilize' Aborigines in schools and mission stations and supported the reintegration of convicts into civil life at the end of their terms: 'it has been My Invariable Opinion', he wrote, 'that, Once a Convict has become a Free Man, either by Servitude, Free Pardon, or Emancipation, he should in All Respects be Considered on a Footing with every other Man in the Colony'.

The character and policies of different governors dominated the early politics of the Australian colonies because of the lack of elected assemblies and the fact that councils, where they existed, were largely nominated by governors. Governors differed considerably in their policies. Ralph Darling, for example, was notable in the late 1820s for his strict oversight of felons in New South Wales, including the use of convicts in chain gangs to carry out government works. At the same time, Lieutenant-Governor George Arthur set about making Van Diemen's Land an efficient gaol for convicts, establishing the notorious Port Arthur penal settlement in 1830. He also pursued a policy of martial law against Aborigines, but his 'Black Line' – a military attempt to remove Indigenous people to peninsulas – was unsuccessful. Not all colonial governors pursued autocratic, draconian policies. The Irish Anglican Richard Bourke, for instance, was a liberal governor of New South Wales in the mid-1830s who oversaw the Church Act of 1836 that granted state support and recognition to the major denominations and provided equal funding for the

Anglicans, Catholics, and Presbyterians. This was a more progressive policy than existed in Britain, where connections between the established Church and the state were still strong. Bourke's Church Act meant that Nonconformist denominations and Catholics in Australia were not reduced to an inferior status. However, Bourke was more severe than liberal in his policy on convicts.

The governor ruled New South Wales solely until 1823, when a parliamentary act created a small council appointed in Britain to consider laws proposed by the governor and to raise taxes. The governor was supported by a small group of officials, including the colonial secretary. From 1823, a chief justice, independent of the governor, determined whether proposed laws conformed to British practice and a Supreme Court oversaw judicial procedures. In 1842, the British government permitted a partly elected legislative council in New South Wales: one-third of the members were appointed and two-thirds elected. The council could, with the governor's approval, pass laws on some matters (but not on land policies, which remained the preserve of Britain). Before 1850 Van Diemen's Land, South Australia, and Western Australia also had governors but their councils were entirely nominated. Many Australian colonists wanted greater political rights in the 1830s and 1840s, but the British government acted cautiously to preserve the status quo until the convict era had ended in eastern Australia and settlements had matured sufficiently for self-government to be considered.

Self-government and the birth of democracy

By the time of the gold rush, many Australians had long wanted to achieve self-government. A minority hoped that political change might go further. Thus the Presbyterian minister John Dunmore Lang, who founded the Australia League in 1850, wanted a republic that upheld 'freedom and independence for the golden lands of Australia'. But most of his fellow subjects wanted to replicate British parliamentary institutions and extend the franchise to most adult males. The British government allowed Tasmania, South Australia and Victoria (after its separation from New South Wales) to have councils from the early 1850s. More important, however, was Britain's decision to grant responsible government to the Australian colonies in 1852. This coincided with a decision to end convict transportation to Van Diemen's Land. Britain considered that Australian society had now entered a phase of consolidated free settlement and that the growth and spread of settlers in Australia was the right time for a shift in the type of government in the Antipodes.

During the 1850s, all Australian colonies except for Western Australia made important political strides by drawing up written constitutions, arranging for bicameral legislatures, and extending the franchise. This was made feasible by the Australian Colonies Government Act (1850). The written constitutions were drawn up by the legislative councils. They provided for a form of representative and responsible government, with the ministry responsible to the parliament and formed by a premier. By the end of the 1850s, New South Wales, Victoria, Tasmania, Queensland (a new colony), and South Australia had all individually established these new forms of government. The new arrangements were more progressive in some respects than existed in Britain. All five colonies mentioned had introduced a secret ballot at elections by 1859, whereas such a voting procedure was not introduced at general elections in Britain until 1872. By 1858, New South Wales, Victoria, and South Australia had secured adult male suffrage for their legislative assemblies. In Britain, by contrast, adult male suffrage at general elections did not occur until immediately after the First World War. Despite these progressive features of the early years of self-government in the Australian colonies, the political system was still restricted in important ways: there was no payment for members of Parliament and the upper houses were dominated by men of wealth and property.

Australia's colonies advanced to a more democratic position in the last four decades of the 19th century. Payment of members was a vital step in this process. This was achieved throughout Australia by 1900, when Western Australia became the last colony to secure this provision. Ordinary men of political inclinations and talent could now take up politics as a vocation whereas previously this had been impossible unless one had an independent income. In securing payment for politicians in the lower houses of the colonial parliaments, there was strong desire for democratic accountability. And that was made more possible than in Britain at this time by the absence of an entrenched landed interest or a hereditary aristocracy in the southern hemisphere. By 1901, the colonial parliaments had reduced the provision for plural voting, whereby wealthy men were able to cast their votes in every constituency in which they owned property.

Politics in the Australian colonies was further influenced by a desire for democracy. In 1854, protesters at the Eureka stockade, near Ballarat, discussed their political rights and indicated, on a small-scale, their capacity for united action: 'We swear by the Southern Cross [a flag with five pointed stars] to stand truly by each other and fight to defend our rights and liberties!' was the diggers' defiant oath sworn on 30 November 1854. Though the revolt was swiftly put down by the military forces, the desire for greater popular participation in politics increased. Trade unions proliferated for skilled labour. Some were based in particular colonies. Others had members throughout the colonies associated with specific occupations. By the 1870s and 1880s, sheep-shearers, wharf labourers, miners, timber-getters, carters, and sailors all had their unions. Many of these bodies were particularly strong in the large colonial capital cities. Melbourne's Trades Hall, still standing on Lygon Street, served as the symbolic base for these groups.

Trade unions benefited from the large proportion of manual workers in Australia, but they struggled to have their voices heard and their concerns acknowledged by the colonial parliaments.

Australian trade unions were proud of their efforts to limit excessive working hours. Though there were factory acts limiting work hours by the early years of the 19th century, the unions campaigned for a maximum working day of eight hours under banners with the slogan 'eight hours' labour, eight hours' recreation, eight hours' rest'. This was first achieved in Melbourne. (A maximum eight hours' work per day was achieved nationally only in the 1920s.) The first intercolonial trade union congress was held in Sydney in 1879. The great maritime strike of 1890 involved many trade unionists. In this dispute, wharf labourers, one of many groups of workers on strike, were defeated by shipowners using non-union workers and the refusal of colonial parliaments to intervene in the dispute.

Women played a significant role in Australia's politics in the late 19th century. Feminist groups met frequently after the mid-1870s to contest the exclusion of women from political life. The impetus towards gaining votes for women came initially from the Victorian Women's Suffrage Society, founded in Melbourne in 1884. This group campaigned for women to have the same voting rights as men. Similar groups had emerged in other Australian colonial capital cities by the end of the 1880s. Influenced by the temperance movement in Britain and the United States, suffragists wrote and distributed leaflets, held meetings and debates, and spread the message that women deserved equal political rights to men. The existing situation, as was then common throughout much of the English-speaking world, was that women were expected to raise families and undertake domestic duties rather than to become involved in public life. The Sydney-based feminist publisher Louisa Lawson succinctly summed up this situation when she wrote that 'men govern the world and the schemes upon which all our institutions are founded show men's thoughts only'.

Supporters of votes for women achieved a major goal in 1894 when South Australia became the second jurisdiction in the English-speaking southern hemisphere, after New Zealand the previous year, to grant female suffrage. The legislation to amend the South Australian Constitution stated succinctly that 'the right to vote for persons to sit in Parliament as members of the Legislative Council, and the right to vote for persons to sit in Parliament as members of the House of Assembly, are hereby extended to women'. Western Australia followed in 1899. The last state to offer female suffrage was Victoria in 1908. Female suffrage for federal elections was achieved throughout Australia in 1902.

Australia was the first country in the world to grant women the right to vote in federal elections and the right to be elected to Parliament. But these gains were only achieved after considerable struggle. In 1891, a few women, including Vida Goldstein and Annette Bear-Crawford, had to call on individual households to gain 30,000 signatures to append to a petition for female suffrage presented to Victoria's Parliament. The next large petition on the subject was gathered in South Australia in 1894 only after three bills attempting to promote female suffrage had been turned down. Women were not eligible to sit in the state parliaments until after the First World War. In 1921, in Western Australia, Edith Cowan became the first woman elected to a state legislative assembly.

Australian women largely channelled their efforts into non-party organizations such as the National Council of Women and the Australian Federation of Women Voters. The first women elected to the Commonwealth Parliament (in 1943) were Enid Lyons of Tasmania and Dorothy Tangney of Western Australia. By 1969, there were only two women in the federal Parliament and very few in the state legislatures. Feminists turned to the world stage to network with international women's organizations and as early delegates to the League of Nations. Jessie Street was a member of the Australian delegation to the United Nations Association conference in San Francisco in 1945, though she played no role in the negotiations there. She was later vice-chairman of the UN Status of Women Commission.

Australian feminists were pioneers in public administration in the 1970s and 1980s, taking up key bureaucratic positions in the federal and state public service as 'femocrats' who related politics and policy issues to the concerns of the women's movement. Despite the low profile of women in party politics, every state except South Australia has had one woman as premier (all representing Labor interests). As of December 2009, women held sixty-eight of the 226 seats in both houses of Australia's federal Parliament. In 2010, Julia Gillard was elected the first female prime minister of Australia.

Individual Australian colonies had a strong sense of their separate identities and rivalries in the later 19th century. Squabbles emerged over commercial regulations, borders, customs arrangements, and quarantine control. Trade and tariff tensions were particularly strong between New South Wales and Victoria, the two most populous colonies. This was reflected in the urban rivalry between Sydney and Melbourne. New South Wales followed a policy of free trade, while Victoria favoured protection: each colony believed its policy was superior. Increasingly, colonies needed to liaise over these and other matters: 83 intercolonial conferences were held between 1860 and 1900. They included the first intercolonial conference of Colonial Chambers of Commerce and Industry, which pressed for uniform legislation on commercial matters, and an intercolonial conference in Sydney in March 1896, which agreed to extend restricted immigration to all coloured races. The rivalry between colonies did not disappear despite these attempts to resolve differences.

Nationalism and Federation

On 1 January 1901, Australia became a nation state under a British Parliamentary Act that created the Commonwealth of Australia. This was the result of a lengthy, and sometimes contentious, move towards Federation that had begun in the late 1880s. By that decade, the representative political institutions granted under self-government had proven durable and the

5. The Australian flag

Australian colonies seemed to have achieved a degree of political and social maturity. By the late 19th century, most people living in Australia had been born there, an essential fact that underpinned those who sought a national identity for a large continent. The nationalism preferred at the time was conceived mainly within an Anglo-Australian framework. Trade unionists, such as those in the pastoral and maritime industries, and feminist supporters of women's suffrage, such as the Victorian Women's Suffrage Society, realized their political goals could be better achieved if Australia's colonies were united as a nation. Publications such as the weekly *Bulletin*, which carried the poems and stories of Henry Lawson and 'Banjo' Paterson, popularized the national destiny of Australians. It was widely accepted that an Australian nation would be a federal polity, with political power and institutions distributed between a national government and the states.

By the late 1880s, a spokesman for a united nation had emerged in the form of Sir Henry Parkes, a former Chartist and premier of New South Wales on five occasions. Parkes's stirring oratory, physical presence, and political experience meant that his views were widely publicized and influential. He wanted to call New South Wales 'Australia' in 1888, but this idea was dropped because it was ridiculed. In the following year, Parkes expressed his enthusiasm for a federated Australia, believing that people scattered across a vast continent could be brought together politically for the benefit of all. In a speech at Leichhardt, Sydney, in 1889, Parkes argued that:

> Australia as a whole, under one great Australian government, representing the people of all this territory, should act for the whole... and do what no one colony could do, and what there was no hope of the several colonies doing in combination... this could be done without in any way wrenching upon the powers and liberties of the separate colonies as they now existed.

In Victoria, another leading spokesman for Federation came to the fore. Alfred Deakin, a lawyer and politician in the Victorian Parliament, and a leading member of the Australian Natives' Association, a voluntary association of those colonists born in the country, made speeches on Federation. Parkes and Deakin played important roles at early conferences dealing with Federation. Deakin attended the first Colonial Conference in London in 1887, where he became convinced that Australia's colonies should speak with one voice. Parkes persuaded Australia's six colonial premiers to meet at a federation conference in Melbourne in 1890, at which Deakin was the youngest delegate. The conference agreed that a united Australia should follow the successful federal example of the USA as an English-speaking democracy covering a continent. But the conference also decided that the British parliamentary system should be retained.

At a federal convention in Sydney in 1891, with representation from each Australian colony and New Zealand, Parkes spoke about the importance of a common people and a common destiny, and suggested that the nation be called the Commonwealth of Australia rather than the United States of Australia. New

Zealand's representatives subsequently withdrew from the discussions because they feared being dominated by Australia. Delegates decided that the government of Australia should blend the British parliamentary and US federal systems. The colonial parliaments would become state parliaments, and there would be a bicameral legislature – an upper house called the Senate and a lower house called the House of Representatives. There would be a written constitution, interpreted by an Australian High Court; but, unlike the United States, there would be no president. Queensland's premier, Samuel Griffith, drafted such a constitution while the debates were in progress, but the colonial parliaments failed to adopt it. Severe economic depression stalled further progress towards Federation.

In 1893, delegates from the Australian colonies reconvened for an unofficial conference at Corowa, a small town in New South Wales. There it was decided that the draft constitution should be revised and that the people – following the US model – should elect representatives from the colonies to form a constitutional convention which would design a constitution to be offered to the people for ratification. The Corowa plan was adopted unanimously. Premiers of individual colonies discussed the plan at Hobart in 1895. They confirmed their acceptance of the proposals. The premiers advocated a White Australia that restricted immigration from Asian countries. They decided that Aboriginals should not be part of the Australian constitution and should not have voting rights.

The Corowa plan was adopted and delegates elected to a new federal convention, which held sessions at Adelaide (1897), Sydney (1897), and Melbourne (1898). Western Australia's parliament chose its delegates rather than put them up for election. Queensland did not attend the convention. Most of the discussion at Adelaide was concerned with specifying the powers of the new federal government. It was agreed that all women should have the right to vote in a federal Australia and that large and small states should have equal representation in the Senate. The remaining contentious issues were thrashed out at the Melbourne session. It was agreed that trade between the states would be free. It was decided that the constitution, redrafted as the Melbourne meeting proceeded, could only be altered by a referendum with a majority of the people and the states.

Many of these issues were fiercely debated. Divisions surfaced between New South Wales's free trade and Victoria's protectionist policies. Western Australia isolated itself from the other colonies by making demands particular to its outlying geographical position, such as a transcontinental railway as a condition of Federation. Labor interests were not for the most part opposed to Federation in principle. They were mainly opposed to the draft bills on offer in 1891 and then again in 1898–9. Their objections were often based on democratic rather than socialist arguments; in other words, the bills were insufficiently democratic because they proposed that each state, regardless of population, would have equal voting rights in the federal senate. But Labor's reservations had limited impact. After two rounds of voting by the people, five colonies ratified the constitution by 1899. Western Australia stood alone, harbouring separatist sentiment, but agreed to federate at the last moment, in June 1900.

Throughout the entire Federation process, Britain largely stayed aloof from the debates but its government realized the administrative convenience of dealing with a central authority rather than six individual governments in Australia. It had been agreed that Britain's constitutional role would be recognized by having a governor-general as the Crown's representative in Australia. Britain, as the ultimate political authority for the Australian colonies, had the right to discuss the plans for Federation. Its main concern was for the integrity of imperial law. In 1900, delegates of the Australian colonies met in the Colonial Office, London, where the issue of appeals to the Privy Council from Australian courts was discussed. Britain then accepted

Australian Federation. The Imperial Parliament now enacted the constitution and the path was clear for the creation of the Australian nation. The inauguration ceremony for the new Commonwealth of Australia, at Sydney's Centennial Park in January 1901, was dominated by smartly dressed Australians and visiting British imperial officials in their regalia and finery. Aborigines were absent and forgotten at the event.

6. Federation Pavilion, Centennial Park, Sydney

Melbourne became the initial capital of federated Australia, with members sitting in Victoria's imposing Parliament House. But it was intended that Australia should have its own purpose-built capital. Owing to the long-standing rivalry between Sydney and Melbourne, and the equal claims of each city to be regarded as Australia's southern metropolis, it was decided that a new site for a capital should be found sufficiently far from each city. In 1909, Canberra was selected, in bush country carved out of New South Wales as the Australian Capital Territory (ACT), which was created in 1911. The American architect Walter Burley Griffin won a competition for the design of the federal capital in 1912, but building was delayed by the First World War. It was not until 1927 that the federal Parliament was located in the city of Canberra, in the ACT, and the Australian government transferred there. The ACT, like the Northern Territory, is self-governing and led by a chief minister.

Australia's political democracy includes distinctive elements. Three noteworthy features are alternative voting procedures, proportional representation voting for the Senate, and compulsory voting. The alternative voting system for federal elections was introduced in Australia in 1918. It entails electing one winner from a pool of candidates using preferential voting. All preferences have to be marked to cast a valid ballot. Australian political parties distribute the party's preference ordering to voters. In recent years, the alternative voting procedure has significantly affected some outcomes, notably the Labor Party victories at the 1990 and 2010 federal elections. The system of proportional representation used for seats in the Senate requires candidates to secure a specified quota of the vote; additionally, parties are allocated seats in proportion to the percentage of the vote they receive. Concerns about the relatively low turnout at elections led, in 1924, to Australia implementing a system of compulsory voting under which fines can be meted out to eligible citizens who fail to vote. Compulsory voting means that voters now comprise 95% of the electorate. Neither the alternative vote nor compulsory voting is particularly popular in Australia, but neither is especially controversial – there is a broad consensus in favour of both, notably the alternative vote (called preferential voting in Australia). Supporters of the compulsory vote regard it as a civic duty and an accurate reflection of the electorate's will. Detractors view it as an infringement of individual liberty and a device for forcing those without political interests to vote.

Political parties

Political parties operate at both federal and state level in Australia. This discussion will concentrate on their federal position. The oldest organized political party is the Australian Labor Party (ALP), formed in 1900 from labour parties that had emerged in New South Wales, Victoria, South Australia, and Queensland in 1890–1. The party originally drew upon blue-collar support in the inner suburbs of the colonial capital cities as well as working-class communities in coal-mining and wheat-belt areas of New South Wales. But over the past half-century the ALP has also drawn support from educated, progressive Australians and public sector workers. The link with the trade unions is solidified in the working of a peculiarly Australian institution – the Court of Conciliation and Arbitration, later called the Australian Industrial Relations Commission, and now a division within Fair Work Australia. Founded in 1904, this is the place where disputes over work conditions and pay are settled. This mechanism has tended to downplay the element of class struggle and collective bargaining because workers' demands are, in theory, arbitrated through an independent body rather than determined by industrial action.

Originally, the ALP was a radical, nationalist party, though it played little part in the coming of Federation. In the 1920s, it was a 'democratic-socialist' party, but since the 1960s, it has become more aligned to social democratic aims and objectives. For most of its history, the ALP has pursued a moderate political agenda:

direct attacks on the capitalist system have been few and far between. It has favoured pragmatic politics, focusing on reforms rather than ideological dogma. Labor tried to nationalize all domestic airlines and banks in the 1940s, but this failed to happen. Nonconformists and Roman Catholics have always been attracted in significant numbers to the ALP, but whereas this once caused division among Labor ranks there is now much less sectarian bitterness within the party.

Caucus and the party platform are important in the ALP. The leader of the ALP is elected by Caucus, which until recently also elected ministers. This form of political organization is an efficient means of mobilizing votes, but it has some potentially undesirable outcomes for the electorate. One is to minimize independent political judgement in favour of the party machine. Another is that factions thrive within the Caucus system; when entrenched, these can prove an impediment to policy changes. Since the 1970s, formal factions have existed in the Labor Party. At one end of the spectrum is the Socialist Left, which generally favours state intervention in the economy and is progressive on social issues; at the other end is Labor Unity (or Labor Right), which aligns itself more with free-market policies and takes a more restrained stance on social affairs. The trade unions are also split into factions.

Since its inception, the ALP has governed for relatively limited periods. Australia's first majority Labor government – the first one in the world – came to office in 1910. By 1915, the ALP governed the Commonwealth as well as five states. In 1916, the Labor Party split over conscription after Prime Minister William M. ('Billy') Hughes lost the first of two referenda on the issue. The ALP struggled at federal level during the 1920s. A short-lived Labor government under James Scullin failed to deal successfully with unemployment and a weakened economy during the Great Depression between 1929 and 1931, and there was a further split. After the fall of Scullin's government in 1931, Labor did not regain power until John Curtin's wartime government a decade later, followed by Ben Chifley's administration in the immediate post-war years. The Curtin–Chifley governments oversaw an ambitious programme of post-war reconstruction and increased immigration to Australia. There then followed a long period in the political wilderness for the ALP until the early 1970s. During the 1950s, when Labor was in opposition, considerable internal party discord occurred from divisions caused by Catholic Actionists and from those who opposed them. The formation of the Democratic Labor Party (the DLP) in 1955 caused problems for the ALP. By directing its preferences to the Liberal Party at subsequent elections, the DLP kept Labor out of office.

The ALP returned to power in the early 1970s after being in opposition for 23 years. Gough Whitlam's Labor government of 1972–5 undertook a whirlwind of social and political measures including greater recognition for Indigenous rights, an end to the White Australia Policy, the official embrace of multiculturalism as government policy, and fuller participation of women in politics. But in late 1975, beset by economic difficulties and a period of three weeks in which the Senate and House of Representatives were at loggerheads over a Supply Bill, the governor-general of Australia, Sir John Kerr, dismissed Whitlam's government and installed Malcolm Fraser, the Liberal leader of the Coalition with the Country Party, as caretaker prime minister. This is the only occasion in Australian history when the governor-general has acted in this manner. 'The dismissal', as it became known, infuriated Labor supporters and left a continuing political resonance.

The ALP had an extended spell in opposition until the emergence of Bob Hawke and successor Paul Keating between 1983 and 1996. Hawke won a record four terms as prime minister. He helped to restructure the role of trade unions and to promote business growth, but at the end of his period in office in 1991 Australia had its highest unemployment rates since the Depression of the 1930s. Keating was provocative in his disdain for the British legacy in Australia. He advocated closer relations between Australia and Asia and held out the prospect of Australia becoming an independent republic. That did not come to pass. After Keating's fall from power in 1996 and a further spell in opposition, the ALP has been returned to power at federal level since 2007 and now rules in a minority government under Julia Gillard.

Political parties opposing Labor in Australia have frequently been reformed to restore their political fortunes. Unlike Britain, there has not been a fully fledged Conservative Party or a party able to command wide support for reactionary policies. The relatively flat social structure of Australia, the prevailing egalitarianism, and the absence of a hereditary aristocracy have ensured that this is the case. In the early years of the 20th century, anti-Labor political forces were staunchly against socialism, especially the more radical variety influenced by imported left-wing ideas from other continents. Anti-Labor political interests were concerned to support property and its rights; they set great store by home-ownership and gained natural support from employer organizations. But they were not exclusively on the side of the private sector: they accepted that a balance should exist between state and private enterprise.

Anti-Labor groups were supported by many white-collar workers, professions, and small business workers, and by rural graziers and pastoralists protective of their rights. After the ALP split over conscription in the First World War, anti-Labor ranks were swelled by returned Anzacs. The Returned and Services League (RSL) became a bastion of these interests. A strong element of Protestant solidarity against Labor's Catholic membership was also manifest among Labor's opponents, though this has now diminished. An essential component of anti-Labor parties was their adherence to independence of voting by members and supporters. The Liberal Party, formed in 1944, has upheld these views. Though party discipline is tightly observed in Australian politics today, Liberal members are not pledged to vote with the party, whereas in the ALP it is obligatory.

Anti-Labor parties have held political power in Australia more frequently than the ALP, but have invariably relied upon political alliances and compromises to govern. There were two anti-Labor political groups immediately after Federation, the liberal protectionists and the conservative free-traders. In 1909, Deakin merged his liberals with the free trade party in order to defeat the ALP and form a government. Hughes's break with the ALP after the 1916 conscription referendum led to a coalition of the newly constituted National Labor government with the Liberals to form the Nationalists. Further conservative realignments occurred. At the end of the First World War, the Country Party emerged as a political force for family farmers and rural voters, who formed a Coalition with the Nationalist Party in 1923. A compromise was reached in which manufacturers were supported by tariffs and farmers helped by bounties. Between 1923 and 1929, this coalition held power through an alliance forged between the Nationalists' leader Stanley Melbourne Bruce, an Anglophile Melbourne businessman, and Earle Page of the Country Party.

After the demise of the Scullin government, a new anti-Labor party, the United Australia Party (UAP) governed Australia, first under the emollient leadership of Joseph Lyons, who oversaw a national economic recovery, and then under the more thrusting presence of a firm Anglophile, Robert Gordon Menzies. The UAP was a fusion between the Nationalists and conservative ex-ALP members. It restored the coalition with the Country Party. Menzies succeeded Lyons in 1939 but following the 1940 election had a narrow majority that depended on the support of independents. Menzies was forced to resign as prime minister when the two independent parliamentarians defected to Labor in 1941. He spent eight years in opposition, during which time he founded the Liberal Party in 1944 as a centre-right replacement for the UAP. The Liberal Party has remained the major anti-Labor party in Australia, though it collaborates with the National Party (formerly the Country Party).

Menzies became prime minister for a second time in 1949, remaining in office for sixteen years – a record for an Australian leader. His government was professional and pragmatic, with little emphasis on ideology. In his radio talk 'The Forgotten People' (1942), Menzies espoused his belief in the enterprise and ambitions of the middle class, who 'are constantly in danger of being ground between the upper and the nether millstones of the false class war; the middle class who, properly regarded, represent the backbone of this country'. This entailed support for white-collar respectability and property, a concern for social justice and national power, and opposition to socialism. Menzies handled crises deftly on the whole. He attempted to ban Communism in Australia, but a referendum in 1951 rejected this course of action. Menzies' government benefited from the economic buoyancy of the 1950s, which included high levels of employment, large-scale immigration, and high export prices, and from internal divisions in the ALP, which produced a divided opposition. After Menzies retired in early 1966, a succession of short-lived Liberal ministries followed before the long post-war years of Liberal dominance ended.

Since the 1970s, there have been two lengthy Liberal governments in Australia, led by Malcolm Fraser (1975–83) and John Howard (1996–2007). Fraser won a majority at three general elections. He grappled with difficult economic times arising from the 1973 oil crisis and, in his final ministry faced tough negotiations with trade unions over wages and employment. Fraser was committed to multiculturalism, welcoming the growth in Asian immigration to Australia and supporting Aboriginal claims for land rights in the Northern Territory. His command over his party was challenged towards the end of his period in government and he lost the 1983 election to Labor. The Liberal Party then spent 13 years in opposition, and Fraser was blamed by his own political colleagues for this period in the political wilderness.

John Howard's government thought multiculturalism had gone too far and that a return to conservatism would serve Australia well for the future. Howard favoured an Australian social fabric based on cohesion, by which he largely meant preservation of the predominant Anglo-Celtic culture. He espoused free-market economics, and the Liberal Party became notably more conservative under his leadership. Howard supported the United States' foreign policy interventions in the Middle East, sending Australian troops to support the invasion of Iraq in 2003. His final years in power included bitter political divisions over alterations to employer–employee relationships under Work Choice arrangements. These proposed fundamental changes to work practices were opposed by trade unions and by many Australians, and contributed to Howard's electoral defeat in 2007.

Aboriginal rights

Aborigines had the right to vote in some Australian colonies, but Queensland in 1885 followed by Western Australia in 1893 debarred them from voting. The creation of the Australian nation in 1901 was concomitant with the exclusion of Indigenous people from the right to vote, from citizenship and from the census. When state and federal election rolls were standardized in 1922, Aborigines were excluded from the franchise. Legislation in 1949 confirmed those on state rolls could vote as well as those who had served in the armed forces. All were enfranchised in 1962. The success of the Civil Rights movement in securing advances for black people in the United States influenced this change. In Australia itself, the work of Aboriginal activists was also important. Harold Holt's Liberal government held a national referendum in 1967 on whether the Commonwealth should be given the power to legislate for Indigenous Australians. Voters overwhelmingly supported this major political change. The inclusion of Indigenous groups in national politics was so limited by the early 1970s, however, that activists set up tents with an Aboriginal flag on the lawn outside Old Parliament House, Canberra, as an alternative parliament called a Tent Embassy.

A major concern of Aboriginal groups lies in securing land rights. Two centuries of settler expansion throughout Australia led to pastoralists and mining companies operating businesses on lands that had ancestral, sacred significance for Indigenous people. The Aboriginal Land Rights (Northern Territory) Act (1976) was the first legal recognition of the Indigenous system of land-ownership. It granted freehold title to Aboriginal groups to hold land that had previously been 'reserves'. Two landmark legal decisions of the 1990s were also important. The Mabo judgment issued by the Australian High Court in June 1992 recognized for the first time that native title existed in parts of Australia and that Indigenous inhabitants were rightful owners of the soil. This implicitly contradicted the European colonizers' understanding that Australia was *terra nullius*, but the legal decision only covered vacant Crown land, national parks, and some leased land. Some state governments refused to cooperate over national legislation dealing with new land leases and compensation payments to Aboriginal communities.

In 1996, in the Wik judgment between the native Wik peoples and the Queensland government, judges ruled that native title and pastoral leases could coexist but that leases did not necessarily annul native title. This blurred the situation over the entitlement, occupation, and use of land. In the late 1990s, the Liberal government was unsympathetic to the implicit advance to Aboriginal rights operative in the Wik judgment, and it spent two years drafting legislation to protect owners of mining and pastoral leases. Howard summed up his government's attitude on the matter by stating that 'the pendulum had swung too far towards Aborigines and had to be reset'. In 1999, Howard moved a 'Motion of Reconciliation', which expressed 'deep and sincere regret that Indigenous Australians suffered injustices under the practices of past generations'. Mounting evidence about violence, health problems, and sexual abuse in Aboriginal communities led the government to pass a controversial bill in 2007, allowing the federal government to intervene in the Aboriginal affairs of the Northern Territory. On 13 February 2008, Prime Minister Kevin Rudd's Labor government offered an official apology for the treatment of Aborigines by non-Indigenous Australians. Howard was the only living Australian prime minister who was absent on that occasion.

Towards a republic?

Arguments that Australia should be a republic were made in the late 19th century. Republican sympathizers stated their views in magazines such as the influential Sydney-based *Bulletin*. In 1887, a Republican Union was formed in New South Wales. But though republicanism was debated among the educated and professional classes, it never had broad support from Australians before Federation. Thereafter, pro-Republican ideas remained largely in the doldrums for most of the 20th century. The low profile of republicanism in Australia was mainly the result of the success of constitutional arrangements made in 1901 for a peaceful democracy based on Westminster models and the enduring connections between Australia and Britain. Those links were weakening by the 1960s, but there was no immediate move towards republicanism in Australia. In 1976, an opinion poll showed that 39% of Australians favoured a republic; in another poll of 1985, the share had slipped to 30%. Traditionally, Australians of Irish-Catholic descent have been more inclined towards republicanism than people of English Protestant background, but over the past 30 years this sectarian division has diminished. Today, supporters and detractors of republicanism include both Protestants and Catholics. A poll of 1,000 readers of *The Sun-Herald* and *The Sydney Morning Herald*, published on

21 November 2010, found 68% of respondents calling for Australia to become a republic.

Whether Australia should become a republic became a major political issue in the 1990s. Since 1991, the ALP has officially advocated republicanism. The Liberal Party, by contrast, includes both monarchists and pro-republicans. Keating made a commitment to republicanism part of the ALP's electoral manifesto in 1993. The expectation was that a referendum would be held, and that Australia might have a major constitutional change to instal a republic in time for the centenary of Federation in 2001. But the issue proved very contentious. Supporters of a republic argued that Australia should not continue to have a head of state who was already the leader of another nation; that self-determination could only be achieved when the nation elected or appointed its own ruler; and that Australian national identity could only be confirmed by such major political change. Those in favour of retaining the queen as the titular head of Australia argued, on the contrary, that a constitutional monarchy had served Australian political stability well; that the governor-general was now always an Australian and the position had lost its threat to political democracy; and that enduring affection and loyalty existed towards Queen Elizabeth II.

Howard's government gave Australians an opportunity to express their choice over the republican/monarchy divide by convening a constitutional convention in 1998 to consider the matter. Delegates to this body were partly elected and partly appointed by Howard. At a referendum held in 1999, Australians in all states rejected the proposition in favour of a republic. Those disappointed by this outcome claimed, with some justification, that the questions were deliberately worded to steer voters towards such a result. In particular, the major question about whether a new head of state should be a president, and how such a person should be elected, and to whom he or she should be accountable, was specified ambiguously. Howard stated that the outcome of the referendum had settled the matter unequivocally. It is more likely, however, that moves towards an Australian republic will be revived, though they are not currently high on the political agenda. The present prime minister, Julia Gillard, wants Australians 'to work our way through to an agreement on a republic'. To achieve that goal, Australians will need a republic that incorporates wider constitutional reform rather than a narrow focus on the powers of a head of state, and they will have to accept new constitutional arrangements for the rights of all Australians.

Chapter 4
Australia and the world

Previous chapters have discussed Australia's connections with the wider world in terms of immigration, trade, and communications. This chapter examines Australia's foreign policy, security, and defence priorities, and its participation in major international conflicts. Before 1850, the Australian colonies comprised a relatively thinly populated outpost in the South Pacific, with most international ties lying with Britain. Knowledge of Asia was relatively limited, and only a small number of Chinese, Afghans, Indians, or other Asian people lived in Australia. Continental Europe had few connections with colonial Australia, either linguistically or in terms of immigration, save for an enclave of German Lutherans in South Australia (and similar, smaller groups in parts of Victoria and southern Queensland). The United States was known for its political institutions and republicanism, but there was little cultural connection between Australian colonists and Americans. Before 1850, Australia relied upon Britain for army and navy support, but was not threatened in any significant way and therefore did not often call upon these resources.

Matters changed considerably in the period between the beginnings of responsible government in Australia and Federation. In that period, Australia became more aware of Asia and other parts of the world through Chinese immigrants and many other nationalities arriving to prospect for gold in the 1850s. Though neither China nor any other Asian power intended to engage with Australia militarily – most were too weak internally even to conceive of this – many Australians were worried about being flooded by a tide of alien immigrants and several Australian colonies clamped down upon Asian immigration. The fear of an 'awakening China' shifted to concern over Japanese expansionism in the Pacific after Japan won the Sino-Japanese War of 1894–5 and decisively defeated the superior Russian fleet in the straits of Tsushima (between Korea and Japan) on 27–28 May 1905 – a naval battle widely reported in Australia. At the time, this was summed up in the remark that 'the yellow man had taught the white man a lesson that Australians can neglect only at their peril'. The phrase 'yellow peril', encapsulating this sentiment, was coined in the 1890s by Kaiser Wilhelm II after reading an Australian text that China's rise would lead to the decline of Western power and influence in the Pacific. Australia entered the 20th century with fears about its strategic isolation on the edge of Asia.

France acquired Tahiti in 1844 and New Caledonia in 1853, but these developments posed no military threat to Australia. After the Franco-Prussian War of 1870–1, Australia no longer feared the French presence in the Pacific but carefully monitored the expansionist policies of Britain and Germany. Australian colonists wanted, as far as possible, to keep the South Pacific as a British 'lake', and were anxious about German encroachments into that region. From the late 1860s onwards, the Australian colonies regularly requested that the British government should annex Southern Pacific islands. In 1883, the premier of Queensland, Sir Thomas McIlwraith, condemned the acquisition of territory south of the Equator by foreign powers as 'highly detrimental to the safety and well-being of the British possessions and injurious to the interests of the Empire'. No doubt he had Germany in mind, for in that year Bismarck seized the northern part of New Guinea, while Britain secured the southern half, Papua. McIlwraith's own attempt to annexe New Guinea for Queensland was disallowed by the British secretary of state for the colonies on the grounds that a colony had no right to annexe other colonies. Instead, Britain established a protectorate in southeastern New Guinea in 1884. Australian fears about the German presence in the South Pacific declined by the 1890s, by which time it appeared that Germany's colonial empire in the Asia-Pacific region would remain minuscule and Russia was also not a threat.

At the very end of the 19th century, Australians welcomed the American acquisition of Hawaii and the Philippines in the Spanish-American War (1898). This was because a nation based on Anglo-Saxon political and linguistic origins, and one friendly to Australia, had staked a claim to territory in the Pacific and seemed to provide a buffer against Asian encroachment into Australia. American naval power was recognized by Australia in 1908, when Alfred Deakin invited President Theodore Roosevelt to send the 'Great White Fleet' to Australia. This duly took place. In August 1908, American marines paraded before a large crowd in Martin Place, Sydney. The arrival of the powerful US fleet, at a time when Australia did not have its own navy, was seen as a symbolic gesture of unity in the Anglo-Saxon world, a signal to Australia's Asian neighbours that they should remain in Asia. But in this period, as we will see, the imperial ties of Anglo-Australian connections remained paramount.

During the 20th century, Australia's relations with the outside world became more complex. As an independent nation, Australia grappled with responsibility for its own defence and security; a greater threat was posed by Asian countries; and Australia gradually became more reliant on the USA as a superpower. The imperial connection with Britain continued but declined markedly after the Second World War. The frequency of serious international conflicts during the 20th century raised questions about whether Australians were being drawn into other people's wars that had no direct connection with Australia's defence or security, or whether fighting in such wars was necessary to maintain good relations with democratic allies to oppose fascism, communism, and international terrorism. From Federation onwards, the Department of Trade and Customs and the Department of External Affairs played significant roles in Australia's foreign representation. These departments amalgamated in 1987 to become the Department of Foreign Affairs and Trade. Diplomatic missions overseas were slower to develop: in 1940, there were only four – in London, Ottawa, Tokyo, and Washington, DC. Today, however, Australia has over 80 overseas diplomatic missions.

Imperial connections

From the arrival of the First Fleet through to Federation, Australia relied upon Britain for her defence needs. Three companies of marines arrived in Botany Bay in January 1788. They were superseded by the New South Wales Corps, a colonial garrison which remained in Sydney until 1809, when it was recalled. The Corps' average strength comprised 550 men. From 1810 to 1870, the Australian colonies were garrisoned by British army infantry regiments whose main duties were to construct and man fortifications and barracks. These regular units were withdrawn from Australia in 1870. This did not cause much unease, however, because they had never been deployed to defend Australia against external attack. Thereafter, Australia's land defence relied upon voluntary work by the colonial militia. The Australian colonies also depended upon British naval protection. From 1821 onwards, one ship from the East India station was routinely stationed for service at Sydney. The creation of the Australia station in 1859 under the command of a commodore consolidated the defence of Australia's self-governing colonies. Royal Navy ships continued to serve in this capacity through to Federation. At the colonial conference in London in 1887, the Australian colonial governments agreed to pay Britain £126,000 per year for the cost of the Australian naval squadron.

These arrangements for Australia's defence reflected the continuing ties between Britain and Australia, but they did not mean that Australians automatically felt they should support wars in which the mother country was engaged. Thus, Australia offered no troops to help Britain fight Russia and Turkey in the Crimean War (1854). On the other hand, volunteer militia from Australia fought in two wars against the Maori in New Zealand in 1845 and 1860. New Zealand had been annexed by the British government in 1840, and was regarded as similar to Australia in the composition of its settler population. The rising of the Maori against British settler rule was viewed as something that Australians should oppose in support of the mother country. In the second of the Maori wars, in Waikato, 2,600 Australian volunteers joined with imperial army units. By the 1870s and 1880s, British imperial expansion into Africa and India caught the imagination of many people in British colonies. In Australia, Queen Victoria was exalted as a sovereign overseeing the spread of British values to the outside world. As Australia's imperial ties with Britain became ever more pronounced, more regular support was mustered for Britain's wars. Whoever constituted Britain's opponent was automatically the enemy of Australia.

Other people's wars?

The first contingent of Australian troops to support Britain's overseas endeavours came from New South Wales. In February 1885, nearly 800 infantry and artillery men sailed from Sydney to Africa to join British forces supporting Egypt in the Sudan. The Islamic Mahdi had declared a *jihad* against Sudan's Egyptian rulers. Britain dispatched General Sir Charles Gordon to Khartoum to restore order. But the dervishes attacked the British garrison in Khartoum and hacked Gordon to death with their swords. Australians had joined up to fight through patriotic sentiments, wanting to take revenge on the Mahdi's forces. This was the first time that troops from a self-governing British colony had participated in an imperial war. However, the Australian contingent took part in very little fighting during its two months' deployment in the Sudan; it mainly provided guards for a railway being built for the benefit of an Anglo-Egyptian army.

Participation in the Sudanese conflict did not mean that Australian colonists would in future become automatically involved in imperial wars. But, at the end of the 19th century, the great publicity and importance attached to the British attempt to secure their position in South Africa found support in Australia. Thus, Australian troops played their part in the Anglo-Boer (or South African) War between 1899 and 1902. In this high-watermark conflict of British imperialism in Africa, Australia's colonies supplied about 10,000 troops to support the British attempt to control the gold fields of the Rand and to defeat the two Boer republics in Orange Free State and the Transvaal. Australian troops did not serve in their own right; they were always part of forces drawn from Canada, New Zealand, and Britain. The Australians mainly contributed to two extended skirmishes at Elands River (August 1900) and Wilmansrust (June 1901) – both in the Transvaal. Australian gold prospectors in South Africa also joined the Cape colonial units and other unofficial forces to fight the Boers. Just over 500 Australians died in the war from wounds, fatal encounters on the battlefield, or disease, a very small portion of the 100,000 or so casualties among the British and empire forces. British imperial troops defeated the Afrikaners. The war helped to cement imperial defence links between Britain and Australia.

Diggers and Anzacs

Australia's first major military encounter as a nation with the wider world came with the outbreak of the First World War. Four days after the assassination of Archduke Franz Ferdinand at Sarajevo on 28 June 1914 – the immediate trigger for the war – Australians volunteered enthusiastically to support Britain's fight against Germany. Once again, imperial loyalties came to the fore.

The Australian Labor leader Andrew Fisher summed up the general mood in his famous pronouncement that 'Australia would stand beside our own to help and defend Britain to our last man and our last shilling'. On 9 November 1914, an Australian warship sank the German cruiser *Emden* off the Cocos Islands. *The Sydney Morning Herald* stated that:

> Monday, November 9, 1914, is a date that will be remembered with pride by the people of Australia for all time. Australians, indeed, are likely to grow prouder of it as time goes on...it was our first sea fight; and on that day a new Australia was born.

Before the war began, Australia had seen the emergence of the Royal Australian Navy in 1911, designed to act as a fleet unit, if necessary far from home, in an imperial force, and the creation of an Australian military college at Duntroon, on the outskirts of Canberra. All Australian males aged between twelve and twenty had had compulsory military training in the four years leading up to the outbreak of the Great War. The volunteer force that sailed from Australian harbours to support Britain in the autumn of 1914 became known as the AIF (Australian Imperial Force). Its engagements during the war were undertaken in conjunction with New Zealanders under the ANZAC heading (Australian and New Zealand Army Corps). Altogether, over 360,000 Australians volunteered for the First World War. They fought in the Middle East, North Africa, and the trenches in Flanders. During the middle of the war, two conscription referenda were held in Australia after Prime Minister Hughes argued that compulsory military participation was necessary to support the Allies in a long-drawn-out war. On each occasion, and with considerable controversy, the referenda returned a 'no' vote.

Australia's role in the First World War was notable for creating an image of brave fighters undergoing a baptism of nationhood through war. The ANZAC participation at the Gallipoli landings made a lasting impact on Australia. In this operation, Australians participated in an amphibious Allied attack on the peninsula adjoining the Dardanelles. This was intended to defeat the Ottoman Empire by capturing Constantinople, thereby severing Turkish support for the Germans and bringing the war on the Eastern Front to a rapid conclusion. The campaign at Gallipoli dragged on from April to December 1915 but ended in failure, with substantial Australian and Allied casualties. It did not achieve any major military objective. This first major Australian contribution to an important world conflict was celebrated for its bravery and loss of life. The day on which the Australians landed on the Gallipoli peninsula, 25 April, has ever since been commemorated as a national day, with an annual ceremony of remembrance. During the war as a whole, Australia lost over 60,000 troops, more than one-in-six of those who had joined up. The fallen are commemorated individually in the names on the walls of the Australian War Memorial, Canberra, completed in 1941, and in many shrines and cenotaphs erected after the war to salute the sacrifice of life and – unlike many of their overseas counterparts – to honour those who served and survived.

The leading Australian war correspondent, C. E. W. Bean, published heroic accounts of the exploits of the ANZACs as a military force, especially at Gallipoli. But while the bravery is properly acknowledged, the myths that arose from the war about Australia's military prowess are exaggerated. Thus, for example, popular accounts of ANZAC highlight the divisions between the British officer class and the rank-and-file Australian soldiers, making a virtue of the down-to-earth independence and abilities of the 'diggers'. But this interpretation runs the risk of over-estimating the uniqueness of the Australian contribution to the conflict: in fact, the discipline and skill of the Australian troops was largely learned from their training in British regular army methods. Today the ANZAC tradition is divisive. On the one hand, it is celebrated by those who want to recall the pride of the Australian contribution to the war effort. On the other hand, many Australians are critical of the continued public association of Australia with these military endeavours.

At the Versailles peace conference of 1919, Prime Minister Hughes unsuccessfully tried to persuade the other victorious powers to levy the entire costs of the Great War against Germany. He was successful, however, in defeating Japan's proposal for a racial equality clause to be inserted into the League of Nations covenant. Australia had been wary of Japan's potential military power ever since the Japanese victory over the Russian navy in 1905. Japan underwent rapid modernization and militarization in the 1930s. It seemed to be the most aggressive power in Asia likely to attack Australia at some stage. Accordingly, Australia's politicians kept a close eye on Japan's expansionist aims. Australia had seven million people: Japan had a hundred million. John Latham, Australia's Minister for External Affairs, went on a goodwill mission to the Far East in 1934. During this visit, he warned Japan about its military expansionism and stated that 'if Japan were to go as far as to attempt to land an army in Australia...she would then find that she had in her hands a very lively hornet's nest'.

At the time of this statement, Australia lacked sufficient defence capability to back up this bravado. But the situation changed over the next few years. As Japan invaded China in 1937, intent on becoming the dominant power in East Asia, Australia, despite following the British policy of appeasement in Europe, decided to follow a policy of rearmament that involved building its own military aircraft and expanding the capacity of its navy. When Menzies became prime minister in April 1939, he affirmed Australia's commitment to the British Empire but he was clear about his country's need to secure her own international arrangements for defence and security: 'what Great Britain calls the Far East is to us the near north', and consequently 'in the Pacific Australia must regard herself as a principal providing herself with her own information and maintaining her own diplomatic contacts with foreign powers'.

The outbreak of the Second World War on 3 September 1939 saw Australia react immediately to the Allied war effort. As Menzies succinctly explained in a radio broadcast:

> Fellow Australians. It is my melancholy duty to inform you officially, that in consequence of a persistence by Germany in her invasion of Poland, Great Britain has declared war upon her and that, as a result, Australia is also at war.

The Australian government sent Royal Australian Air Force (RAAF) aircrews and a number of Royal Australian Navy (RAN) ships to fight for Britain. A second AIF was formed, once again comprising entirely volunteers. It served mainly in the North African war in the desert against Italy and then Rommel, notably taking part in the siege of Tobruk (March–December 1941) and the two battles of El Alamein (July, October, and November 1942). The Allied victory at El Alamein led to the German surrender in North Africa in May 1943. Australians also saw combat in fighting against the German invasion of Greece and Crete in 1941 and later fought against German, Vichy French, and Italian opponents in Egypt, Syria, Lebanon, and throughout the Mediterranean. By contrast, Australian troops were only modestly involved in the fighting in Europe. The hardiness and discipline of Australian troops attracted much favourable commentary.

The length and geographical scope of the war necessitated a greater impact on the home front in Australia than had been experienced in the First World War. Under the National Security Act (1940), Australians were required to undergo conscription for the militia at home and the government later introduced rationing and the control of the nation's industrial resources for the war effort. Daylight saving time was introduced. Some European and all Japanese aliens were interned for the duration of the war.

Personal identity cards were issued. Clothing, footwear, tea, butter, and sugar were rationed from 1942. Women were increasingly enlisted into auxiliary forces. By 1942, around half a million Australians were working on munitions, aircraft, war supplies, aerodromes, docks, and roads. In northern Australia, Aborigines were paid to carry out manual work such as digging sanitary sites, manning sawmills, and carting gravel.

During the Second World War, Australia was directly threatened by Japanese military expansionism. The Japanese entry into the war came as a shock to Australians, many of whom had remained insular and cut off from the realities of overseas events. After Japanese bombers destroyed part of the US fleet at Pearl Harbor, Hawaii, on 7 December 1941, Prime Minister John Curtin did not wait to take account of Britain's reaction: he declared immediately that Australia was at war with Japan. He also turned to the United States for military help, stating in an historic article in the Melbourne *Herald* that such aid was needed: 'Without any inhibitions of any kind, I make it clear that Australia looks to America, free of any pangs as to our traditional links or kinship with the United Kingdom.' Several reasons account for Australia's vulnerability to enemy attack. Australia was largely dependent on Britain for naval protection; it had many thousands of miles of unprotected coastline along its northern shores that the Japanese could invade; and its elite troops were mainly on the other side of the world.

Winston Churchill had repeatedly reassured Australia that Britain's leading naval base in Asian waters, at Singapore, would be properly manned and protected, and naval vessels made available for Australia's protection. But by this time, Britain was unable to send the forces needed to defend the Singapore naval base. In February 1942, the Japanese attacked Singapore, taking it by surprise through the jungle of the Malayan peninsula to the north of the naval base. Japan then launched an air attack on Darwin four days later. These actions confirmed Australia's fears of Japan. Singapore was expected to hold out for six months, but Japanese forces captured it in ten days. Some 15,000 Australian servicemen were taken prisoner as a result. Many served out the war either in the notorious Changi prison or constructing the Burma railway. In Australia itself, there were strong fears that defence limitations would lead to the continent being abandoned to invaders above a line, known as 'the Brisbane Line', stretching from Adelaide to Brisbane. This would enable Australia to concentrate resources on southeastern parts of the continent where most of its industrial and munitions resources were located. But claims that such a plan had been adopted to allow large swathes of Australia to fall into Japanese hands were exaggerated.

American military forces first came to Australia in December 1941, having been diverted from the Philippines. General Douglas MacArthur arrived in March 1942 as Allied Supreme Commander in the South-West Pacific after the US decided to make Australia its base in the region. Over the remainder of the war, some one million American troops passed through Australia. Australians and Americans thereafter fought alongside each other. Americans commanded the allied air and naval forces. General Sir Thomas Blamey, who had served with both the 1st and 2nd AIF, was made commander of the army troops, though in fact MacArthur controlled operations. Curtin insisted to Churchill that two Australian divisions be sent home from the Middle East to defend Australia against Japan. A third division was wrested back from Africa in February 1943. Curtin, who had firmly opposed conscription during the First World War, now introduced it for Australians as far north as the Equator.

In 1942, Australian militia were dispatched to fight Japanese troops in New Guinea along the notorious jungle paths of the Kokoda trail. Australian and Americans also joined together in naval and aircraft endeavours against the Japanese. In May and June 1942, at the Battles of the Coral Sea and Midway, Japan was heavily defeated. By the end of the Pacific War in August 1945,

7. **Engineers building a bridge, Kokoda, New Guinea, November 1942**

over half a million Australians were in uniform. Australia lost 34,000 troops during the war. Despite Australia's contribution to the war effort, especially in North Africa and the Southern Pacific, no single military engagement in which they were engaged gained the same iconic status as Gallipoli in the First World War, though Kokoda has since assumed some importance.

From the Cold War to the War on Terror

Australia's reliance on military support from the United States did not break down the Anglo-Australian relationship comprehensively.

Nevertheless, with a weakened British Empire emerging after the Second World War and the consolidation of the USA as a superpower, it was clear that Australia would look to the United States for defence and security help in the immediate future. Suggestions that Australia might run its foreign policy as an independent nation, without help from a superpower, soon proved unrealistic as the shadow of potential nuclear warfare split the world into democratic and Communist regimes during the Cold War. The Soviet Union's attempts to spread Communism into eastern and central Europe were publicized worldwide, and Australia feared that such expansion would spread into Asian countries.

Australia's particular concerns after the end of the Second World War lay in ensuring the Pacific was a peaceful region and that friendly relations were maintained with its Asian neighbours. Immediately after 1945, Australia thought Japan might exact reprisals for its humiliation in the Second World War. This turned out to be an unwarranted fear, and Australia was able to begin withdrawing its occupation forces from Japan in late 1950. Australia established good relations with India and Pakistan after those countries were established in the partition of 1947, and it supported nationalist China, which had been a wartime ally. It helped the Indonesian states to gain independence from Dutch control by lobbying the international forum of the United Nations. Of growing concern, however, as the Cold War progressed, was the fear of Communist influence on Australia from Asian countries. This greatly concerned Australians after the rise of Mao Tse Tung to lead the People's Republic of China (PRC) in 1949 with the support of the Soviet Union, the flight of nationalist Chinese leaders to Taiwan, and the rapid spread of Communist practices to North Korea. The Soviets had turned eastwards where there was no organization such as NATO (North Atlantic Treaty Organization) to oppose their plans for wider influence.

Australia's diplomacy and foreign policy after the Second World War was thus geared towards protection of the Pacific region, with

American help. After 1949, the emergence of the PRC led
Australia to counter Communism in Asia. This involved the search
for agreements and treaties with friendly, non-Communist nations
for mutual support and defensive alliances, and continuing
cooperation with Britain and other Commonwealth nations in
circumstances where mutual interests were shared. Australia and
New Zealand came together with Britain, for example, in an
agreement called ANZAM, whereby Australia and New Zealand
helped Britain to defend the Malayan area. This was put into
effect in 1950 when Australian aircraft were deployed to support
British troops confronting Communist insurgents in Malaya.

Agreements between Australia and British Commonwealth
nations, however, did not always focus on military arrangements.
The Menzies government participated in the Colombo Plan
(1950) whereby the foreign ministers of seven British
Commonwealth countries agreed to support underdeveloped
countries in south-east Asia to improve their living standards and
access to technology as a means of staving off the lure of
Communism. Australia contributed over £31 million in the first
six years of this scheme for cooperative economic and social
development, which led to the building of roads, railways,
airports, dams and fertilizer plants in south-east Asian countries.
The plan also gave opportunities for Asian students to study at
Australian universities and helped to secure technology transfer
between member countries.

Australia could no longer rely on British support for her security
concerns in the Pacific region as Clement Attlee's Labour
government made it clear that the Middle East was a greater
defence concern for Britain than the Pacific. This made it more
vital that Australia should secure a defence agreement with the
United States. Attempts to do so between 1945 and 1949
foundered on Australian attempts to gain access to American
Pacific bases such as Guam and Manus Island and on the United
States finding that it had greater concerns for possible military

deployment in Europe, the Middle East, and North-East Asia rather than the South Pacific. Australia supported the USA in the Korean War, which broke out in June 1950. Australia participated in the war primarily to create a defence pact with the United States. Korea had been occupied by the Japanese during the Second World War, but had been split at the end of the conflict at the 38th parallel: North Korea had become a Communist regime and South Korea had an autocratic and repressive government. The United States led the UN forces that opposed North Korea's invasion of South Korea, and was grateful for military support from Australia. Two years of stalemate in terms of fighting eventually led to an armistice in 1953 that has lasted until today.

The ANZUS Treaty (1951) consolidated Australia's foreign policy connections with the United States. Signed by Australia, New Zealand, and the USA, the treaty specified that members would consult together when any one of them considered their territorial integrity, political independence, or security was threatened in the Pacific. The United States gained Australia's support for a peace treaty with the Japanese in return for participation in the ANZUS alliance. The ANZUS pact signalled Australia's intention that its diplomacy would now be more dependent on Washington, DC, than on London. There was realization that Australia was not a world-class military power. As the South Australian politician R. S. Ryan put it to the federal House of Representatives: 'Australia is a second-class power and the first plank of its policy must be to choose its friends wisely, and having chosen them to gain their goodwill.'

Australia's interest in creating a defensive buffer zone between China and its own shores was further boosted in 1954 with the signing of the South-East Asia Collective Defence Treaty under the auspices of SEATO (the South-East Asia Treaty Organization). Australia, France, New Zealand, Pakistan, the Philippines, Thailand, Britain, and the United States came together in this treaty, binding themselves in a defensive alliance against Communist governments in the region. SEATO was initially stimulated by the fall of French colonial power in Vietnam. Australia believed that the fall of South Vietnam to North Vietnamese Communists in a guerrilla war would lead to the Communist conquest of Cambodia, Laos, and the rest of South-East Asia. A neutral stance was not an option for Australia. Australia's involvement in the Vietnam War after 1962 was the price to be paid for American help over security and defence in the event of Australia being attacked or her Asian neighbours being threatened by Communist insurgents.

Australia began its involvement in Vietnam with a relatively modest commitment of forces. But by 1965, Menzies stated in the Australian Parliament that

> the takeover of South Viet Nam would be a direct military threat to Australia and all the countries of South and South-East Asia. It must be seen as part of a thrust by Communist China between the Indian and Pacific Oceans.

Accordingly, in March 1966, Australia increased the number of troops deployed there to 4,500 in line with the increased American military presence. Britain did not commit troops to the conflict. Thus, for the first time in over a century, Australia took part in a war without Britain. Partial conscription was introduced in Australia in late 1964 to draft sufficient troops for this purpose; it was based on birth dates in a particular year drawn in a ballot.

In July 1966, Prime Minister Harold Holt's visit to President Lyndon B. Johnson in Washington, DC, led to the Australia–United States relationship growing closer: Holt stated that Australia would go 'all the way with LBJ' – an echo of Johnson's election campaign slogan. Johnson's subsequent visit to Australia proved politically divisive, however, leading to many demonstrations in Australia's cities against the Vietnam War. The statement by another Australian prime minister, John Gorton, to US President Richard

M. Nixon that Australia 'will go a-waltzing Matilda with you' further inflamed Australian public opinion on the war. Conscription and Australian participation in the war remained a controversial matter in Australian public life, as indeed in Britain and the United States, until the US–Australian withdrawal from Vietnam in 1972.

The Australian public gradually became disenchanted with the Vietnam War; university students protested vehemently against it; and a major demonstration in all cities took place in May 1970. Media portrayals of the devastation in Vietnam had a sharp impact on public opinion. Whitlam's Labor government, elected in 1972, quickly removed Australian servicemen from an unpopular war. It recognized that the threat from Communist China had been exaggerated, and therefore offered it diplomatic recognition. SEATO came to be regarded as an ineffective body. France and Britain had refused to join Australia and other member countries in the war in Vietnam. At a meeting in New York in 1975, it was decided to disband SEATO, and this duly happened two years later.

An Asia-Pacific destiny?

After the withdrawal of Australian military support for the United States in Vietnam, there was a hiatus in Australian involvement in overseas conflicts. During the 1970s and 1980s, Australia, with an official policy of multiculturalism, was more involved in trade and diplomatic arrangements with a greater variety of nations than had been the case for most of its history. In particular, Australia was forging greater links with Asian countries in terms of immigration, trade, and diplomacy. Vietnamese boat people arrived as refugees in Australia in the late 1970s, and were accepted on humanitarian grounds. Many Asian immigrants came to Australia in the 1970s and 1980s in the wake of the ending of the White Australia Policy. Some 100,000 Asian refugees entered Australia in the decade after 1976. Japan and, to a lesser extent,

China were significant trade partners of Australia. Two-thirds of Australia's exports were sent to Asian countries by the end of the 1980s. In June 1976, the Australian and Japanese governments signed a Treaty of Friendship and Cooperation, the first general bilateral agreement between Australia and an Asian power. This became the model for subsequent treaties with other Asian countries.

The end of the Cold War in 1989 seemed to herald the beginning of a new era of international peace in which the threat of the spread of Communism was diminished and former Communist countries reintegrated into Western notions of democracy. For Australia, this held the prospect of easier relations with some Asian countries. Yet a wary eye was still needed in overseeing nations with proximity to Australia with military regimes in power, such as Indonesia. Australia contributed, via its membership of the United Nations, to UN-sanctioned missions in the Second Gulf War of 1990–1, prompted by the Iraqi invasion of Kuwait, and the intervention in Somalia in 1992–3. The chief Australian military contribution to the Second Gulf War lay in the provision of warships under US operational control. These contributed to the conflict until the end of the ground war and the liberation of Kuwait. Australia suffered no casualties in the war.

Between 1993 and 1996, Australia made a modest contribution to the UN-driven intervention to restore peace to internal warfare in Somalia, sending one battalion group comprising fewer than 1,000 personnel. Australia withdrew its forces from Somalia before security and civil law and order had been properly established, however, because the Commonwealth government had set a strict time limit of 17 weeks for Australian involvement in the crisis. During the 1990s, Australia also had a significant peacekeeping role in Cambodia, where it played a diplomatic role in trying to arrange a peaceful settlement in a country suffering from the aftermath of the genocidal Pol Pot regime in the 1970s.

Australian peacekeeping forces in the 1990s also spread to Rwanda and East Timor.

Paul Keating's period as prime minister (1991–6) saw attempts to increase Australian participation in Asian affairs. He travelled to Asian countries frequently and set up close economic relationships with the governments of South Korea, China, Japan, Vietnam, and numerous countries in the South Pacific. With American support, he continued to support a forum known as Asia-Pacific Economic Cooperation (APEC). This had been established under Hawke's government in 1989. It aimed to move the Asia-Pacific region towards free trade in the decade 2010–20. This would have not only economic benefits, but would bolster Australia's security by firmly establishing cordial relations with Asia-Pacific neighbours. A positive response came from many Asian countries, with the exception of Malaysia where the governing regime did not consider Australia capable of playing a major part in the region's affairs. Keating's relations with Asian countries proved politically divisive, however, at home. He was accused by some Liberal opponents of wanting to make Australia a part of Asia. In a speech of December 1993, Keating attacked this misrepresentation of his policy:

> Australia is not, and can never be, an 'Asian nation' any more than we can – or want to be – European or North American or African. We can only be Australian and can only relate to our friends as Australian.

Indonesia, containing more than ten times as many people as Australia, became the major centre for Australian military involvement with the outside world at the end of the 20th century. The Indonesian army invaded Portuguese Timor in the mid-1970s. Australia tolerated President Sukharto's military regime in Indonesia for over 30 years, but sections of the Australian public were sensitive about his poor record on human rights and harsh treatment of his internal critics. They also criticized Indonesian military repression in East Timor. Sukharto's fall from power in 1998 encouraged the suppressed people of East Timor, immediately to the north of Australia, to seek political freedom and independence. Anarchy resulted in East Timor. The deployment of an Australian peacekeeping force there caused severe diplomatic tensions between the Australian and Indonesian governments.

Ill-feeling was exacerbated through Australian interception of ships containing illegal immigrants dispatched by criminals based in Indonesia who were involved in smuggling people. In a high-profile incident in August 2001, soon before an election campaign, a Norwegian freighter the *Tampa* went to the rescue of a sinking boat with over 400 Afghans seeking asylum in Australia. The Commonwealth government would not allow the refugees to enter Australia's territorial waters; instead most of the refugees were escorted to a Pacific holding camp on the tiny island of Nauru. This caused diplomatic tension between Australia and Norway and controversy with supporters of human rights, who opposed this policy and practice. Further difficulties were caused in October 2001 when the crew of an illegal entry vessel allegedly threw children overboard after being told by the Australian authorities to return to Indonesian waters. This gained extensive publicity during an Australian federal election campaign, but the story was later found to be fabricated. At the time, however, the Australian public was deeply concerned about border-protection measures and many Australians supported the demonization of asylum-seekers. Australia officially remained deeply suspicious of refugees in the first decade of the 21st century, placing many of them in detention centres surrounded by barbed wire, such as at Woomera in the isolated desert country of South Australia.

Australia's policies towards Indonesia and its fear of illegal immigrants bringing radical Islamic views to the Antipodes escalated after the terrorist attacks by al-Qaeda on New York's World Trade Center on 11 September 2001. Prime Minister John

Howard supported the US action in Afghanistan and subsequently to depose Saddam Hussein from power in Iraq, with British support but without the sanction of the United Nations. Australian troops made only a small contribution to the Afghan and Iraq wars, but their participation in those conflicts made Australia a possible target for Islamic militant activity. That this was more than an imagined threat was underlined in 2002, when a terrorist bomb explosion in Bali claimed more than 100 Australian victims. The protracted nature of the war in Iraq and the woeful exit strategy pursued by the Allied forces made it likely, for the foreseeable future, that Australia and her coalition allies would not seek further large-scale unilateral military action in the Islamic world.

Today, Australia preserves its commitment to maintaining stable political and economic relations with its Asia-Pacific neighbours in order to protect its security. Relations with Indonesia have stabilized in recent years. Moreover, Indonesia's weak air and naval forces mean that it does not pose a security risk. Of continuing concern to Australia are weak and failing states. Thus a close eye is kept on key nearby countries such as Fiji, Papua New Guinea, and East Timor. The major larger security concern for the future lies in the rising strength of Asian powers, especially China, as American power over Asia, secured over the past 40 years, is challenged. The prospect of competition between Asian powers such as China, Japan, and India to counteract American hegemony in the Asia-Pacific region, will leave Australia with decisions about whether such changes constitute a greater security risk. The Australian government will need to decide whether defence spending should increase, especially on naval and air forces, in order to maintain Australia's status as a middling power in what seems likely to become the Asian century.

Chapter 5
Body and soul

Australia's climate has always made it a place where outdoors leisure activities are widely undertaken and enjoyed, whether surfing and beach culture or the pursuit of sport, but it also has a long artistic tradition with notable accomplishment in the fine arts, literature, and music. Australia achieved prominence in several sports by the early 20th century. Physical fitness was a priority for Australians, ensuring a regular supply of new athletic talent to replace those who had made their sporting mark but were ready for retirement. Australians, living mainly within reach of the coast, extending for 30,000 kilometres around the continent, have been described as 'the world's greatest beachgoers'. Almost all beaches in Australia are free, and they are often a focal point for family and social gatherings and celebrations: on Christmas Day, for example, it is common for around 40,000 Australians to visit Sydney's Bondi Beach. Since the formation of the Bondi Surf Bather's Life Saving Club in 1907, the surf lifesaver has become an Australian icon. Max Dupain's photographs *Sunbaker* and *Bondi*, both taken in the late 1930s, are well-known visual representations of the Australian beach. By the end of 2007, Australia had more than 37,000 surf lifesavers and a total voluntary membership of 130,000. Nevertheless, the emphasis on sporting pursuits is now under threat in Australia, as in many other Western countries, by an alarming rise in obesity. According to statistics for 2007 from the World Health Organization,

Australia has the third highest incidence of adult obesity in the English-speaking world (with the United States and New Zealand in first and second places).

Australian prominence in the arts emerged more slowly than sporting excellence. For many years, the artistic climate in Australia was considered too dependent on Europe, too derivative of forms pioneered in the Old World, and not stimulating enough to encourage the emergence and sustenance of talent. In the 1890s, Henry Lawson was already lamenting the difficulties of an Australian writer producing work that was genuinely Australian and praised for its artistic merits as a product of the southern hemisphere. Matters did not change significantly for many decades. In 1947, the artist Albert Tucker, one of a group known as the Angry Penguins, left Melbourne on his first overseas trip and announced, 'I am a refugee from Australian culture'. When this remark was made, many observers felt that artistic production in the Antipodes was second rate and derivative rather than independently Australian. In 1950, the literary critic A. A. Phillips coined the phrase 'the cultural cringe', an internalized inferiority complex in which Australians characterized their own nation's culture as inferior to that of metropolitan centres. But that self-criticism has now faded, to be replaced with a strong tradition of Australian cultural achievement.

Popular leisure

Australia is often characterized as an easy-going country in which leisure pursuits are accorded a high priority in most people's lives. This partly stems from favourable climatic conditions for outdoor pursuits and from sufficient leisure time arising from the eight-hour work day. In the early days of white settlement, recreation centred around activities brought over from Britain: holidays at Christmas, Easter, and various saints' days; wakes and fairs; numerous sports such as cricket, football, horseracing, cockfighting, and prizefighting. These pursuits, which lay at the heart of popular culture in pre-industrial England, migrated to colonial Australia. Team sports were initially a minority affair but later became central to Australian social life. Horseracing occurred intermittently in early 19th-century Sydney and Hobart, but became firmly established in all the colonies by the 1830s and 1840s. A permanent institution, the Australian Jockey Club, was founded in 1842. Leisure pursuits transplanted from British origins often attracted people from all classes, with wealthier men acting as patrons to lower-class spectators or participants. But, as in 19th-century Britain, a gulf emerged between genteel and rougher pursuits and upper-class patronage began to disappear. Attacks by evangelicals and respectable professional citizens on sports such as cockfighting and prizefighting, which often overspilled into drunkenness and disorderliness, led to the decline of those pastimes in Australia's colonies by the 1850s.

Between the end of the gold rush era and the First World War, Australian leisure patterns were shaped by the continuance of transplanted British and Irish traditions, by the introduction of some American influences upon popular culture, by the growth of urbanization, and by increased leisure time for ordinary workers made possible by Saturday half-day holidays. Crowd entertainments assumed greater importance in this period. Australian city dwellers were treated to a regular supply of theatre, melodrama, music hall, vaudeville, pantomime, minstrel show, circus, and musical comedy. Large theatres were built in city centres to cater for public demand. Entrepreneurs, such as the J. C. Williamson group, Harry Rickards, and the Fullers, promoted these venues, hired performers to appear in them, and maintained theatrical agents in each city. Ticket prices at such venues were generally modest, enabling working-class Australians to attend.

Britain was the progenitor of musical comedies that flourished in colonial Australia, notably Gilbert & Sullivan operettas such as *The Mikado* and *The Yeoman of the Guard*, which were popular among all ranks of Australians and which have retained their broad audience appeal until today. Britain also largely contributed to the many melodramas, which became the most popular form of theatre in Australia between 1870 and 1914. These plays, usually based on two-dimensional characters with obvious virtues and vices, enabled theatregoers to applaud do-gooders and hiss at villains. The stagey melodramas of the Irish playwright Dion Boucicault were performed more often on the colonial Australian stage than the plays of Shakespeare.

The United States began to influence Australian popular leisure in the later 19th century. Vaudeville, in which a series of short acts followed one another on stage, and minstrelsy, in which white actors 'blacked up' their faces to sing ballads associated with black Americans, were introduced to Australia in the wake of their success in the United States. The establishment of a regular steamship route from San Francisco to Sydney by the 1880s enabled travelling entertainers to visit Australia from the west coast of the United States to promote minstrel shows and Vaudeville entertainment.

Immediately after the First World War, the cinema rapidly replaced Vaudeville, the minstrel show, and music hall. Movies, even in the era of silent films, became an instant popular success: in 1921 in New South Wales, more people attended picture shows than all other forms of theatre combined. Large picture theatres had already been established in the large Australian cities in the years just before the First World War. They were now easily adapted to entertainment provided by the cinema. New cinemas were built in the city centres and suburbs. Some had spectacular interiors, such as Melbourne's State Theatre, with its minarets and coloured domes. There were 1,250 cinemas in Australia by 1928, with an annual attendance of 110 million.

Australia played a pioneering part in the early cinema industry. Indeed, *The Story of the Kelly Gang* (1906) is credited as the first full-length feature film. The 1919 silent film *The Sentimental Bloke* was popular with Australian audiences. Australia made sixty-five feature films in the 1930s. Often based on well-known themes from Australian history, these releases included *The Squatter's Daughter* (1933). The introduction of Hollywood offices in Australia by 1918, however, led to cinemas showing more American movies, though films made in Australia and based around historical events and family relationships found an audience. Over three-quarters of the films shown in cinemas were American-made, even up to the Second World War. Australia, in fact, frequently imported more American films than any other country.

Cinema retained its popularity because of its low prices compared to live theatre, its technological novelty and the availability of cinemas to an urban working population. Hollywood blockbusters such as *Ben Hur* (1960) were popular in Australia. The first Australian colour film was *Jedda* (1955), which featured Aboriginal actors. One of the best-known Australian films of the 1960s was *They're a Weird Mob* (1966), directed by an Englishman, Michael Powell, with an Italian star, Walter Chiari. This was a story of how an Italian newcomer – one of Australia's 'new immigrants' after the Second World War – adopted the Australian way of life.

New technology opened the door for further leisure activities via the emergence of radio broadcasting in the early 1920s. Australia developed a dual system of 'A'-class stations based on documentaries, classical music, and higher culture, and 'B'-class stations that were more middlebrow in content, with popular music and quizzes. The 'A'-class stations became the preserve of the Australian Broadcasting Commission, founded in 1932 in the public service tradition of the BBC in Britain. The 'B'-class stations were supported entirely commercially by advertising revenue. After a modest start in the 1920s, when radio transmission was often poor in quality, most Australian homes acquired a wireless set in the 1930s, when families became accustomed to huddling around the set to listen to broadcasts. There were over 1.2 million radio licence-holders in Australia by 1942. Radio broadcasts included news, sport, serials, and music. By the 1950s, radio featured more quizzes, children's programmes, and a hit parade of popular music.

Television reached Australia much later than in Britain or the United States. The first black-and-white television broadcasts were aired in Australia in 1956; colour television began in 1975. The British model of government-owned broadcasting was partially followed as the ABC became a major network. Many of the ABC's radio and TV programmes until the 1960s were hosted by English expatriates or by Australians imitating a plummy upper-middle-class English accent. Commercial channels also operated from the beginning of TV broadcasting in Australia. Programmes ranged from news and current affairs to quiz shows, sport and popular music. Today there are three main commercial channels – the Nine Network, the Seven Network and Network Ten. Pay television has become more popular in recent years, with more than a quarter of Australian homes having access to these channels by 2005. Australians took to the new medium of television immediately. Cinema attendance was strongly affected. In Victoria alone, cinema attendance fell from 34 million in 1956/7 to 16 million in 1960/1.

Initially, Australian television had home-grown content, but imported Hollywood films and popular shows based on American models became common. The influence of American popular culture on Australian television was also demonstrated in two shows featuring rock 'n roll music by 1959. From the late 1960s onwards, however, the situation changed as more Australian-made programmes became popular. These included police series and dramas such as *The Sullivans* and *A Country Practice* and current affairs bulletins such as *Sixty Minutes* and *Lateline*. From the late 1970s, mini-series were added. *A Town like Alice*, based on

Nevil Shute's bestselling novel, is an example of a popular Australian TV series which was shown internationally. Soap operas, such as *Neighbours* and *Home and Away*, became Australian popular cultural exports by the late 1980s.

In 1970, the federal government boosted Australia's film industry by establishing a Film Development Corporation to fund Australian-made films and television programmes. Period films were made as part of this initiative. Some of them were widely circulated to cinema audiences internationally. Such was the case with *Picnic at Hanging Rock* (1975), a mystery film dealing with a fictitious disappearance by three schoolgirls and their teacher in Victoria in 1900, and *Breaker Morant* (1980), a nationalist attack on the class divide between the British and Australian troops in the Anglo-Boer War of 1899–1902. *Gallipoli* (1981) portrayed the loss of innocence and growing spirit of national identity among Australian military recruits in the failed attack in Turkey during the First World War. Well received within Australia but less well known internationally was *The Man from Snowy River* (1982), which focused on the rugged bushmen and Australian outback scenery. *Crocodile Dundee* (1986) attracted international audiences. Its appeal lay in humorous stereotypes of the rugged, wisecracking Australian male character. The Australian cinema industry has continued to produce high-quality films, but many leading actors and actresses are increasingly drawn across the Pacific from Australia to pursue fame and fortune in Hollywood.

The sporting tradition

Australia has a proud sporting tradition. Australians have embraced numerous sports, such as swimming, horseracing, golf, tennis, and many team games. Australians are known for their sharp-elbowed competitiveness and their desire to win: sporting wins are often equated with national success. Australia's best sportsmen and -women have long made their mark internationally. Australia's sporting prowess has also been presented to the world at Olympic and Commonwealth Games. Australia has hosted two successful Olympic Games, in Melbourne (1956) and Sydney (2000). At the Melbourne Games, the swimmer Dawn Fraser won the 100-metre women's freestyle in record time. Altogether, Fraser won four gold and four silver medals for swimming at different Olympic Games. Australia is regularly one of the five best-performing countries at the Games.

Many of Australia's popular team sports originated from games imported from Britain. This is true of rugby union and rugby league, which have strong followings in New South Wales, Queensland, and the ACT; and of cricket, which is played throughout Australia. Association football, a game with a wider following in Britain than either of the rugby codes, has been slower to achieve popularity in Australia. Apart from the use of technology and the marketing and advertising of sports events, all of which have expanded since the end of the Second World War, American influence on sports played in Australia has been relatively minor, though baseball and basketball – both staples of US sporting culture – became popular in Australia. Baseball's popularity, however, is now in decline. In most respects, Australian sport has remained an offshoot of games originally derived from Britain and Ireland.

Rugby Union and Rugby League, as in Britain, have largely attracted different groups of players and supporters in Australia. Rugby Union traditionally drew upon a more diverse social group of players than Rugby League. Rugby Union had a gentlemanly tradition based on privately educated young men, whereas Rugby League was associated with tight-knit working-class communities as befits a code of the game originating in the northern industrial towns of Britain. There are other differences, too: Union has fifteen players while League has thirteen; Union has line-outs and kicks to touch from one's back quarter while League has neither; Union has rucks and mauls whereas League has a six-tackle rule before a pass has to be made. Union has for most of its history been an amateur game whereas League has been professional since 1907–8.

Rugby Union in Australia first flourished in the Sydney area in the 1860s. Clubs in and around the city organized themselves into the Southern Rugby Football Union in 1891. They attracted fairly small crowds except when international matches were played. Rugby Union's amateur status remained in place in Australia until the 1990s when the game turned professional. Thereafter, players, instead of a part-time commitment for which they could be reimbursed expenses, played in professional leagues. Today, the major matches that attract crowds, advertising, and television companies to Rugby Union are internationals against major rivals such as South Africa, New Zealand, France, England, Wales, Scotland, and Ireland. Australia won the quadrennial World Cup in 1991 and hosted the tournament in 2003, when England defeated Australia in the final.

Rugby League had established solid working-class support in inner-city suburbs by the outbreak of the First World War. It continued to flourish between the two World Wars and attracted large crowds to international fixtures against Great Britain. After experiencing some decline in support in the 1950s, Rugby League revived and broadened its supporters with the arrival of televised club games from 1961 and live broadcasts of the annual Grand Final from 1967 onwards. Rugby League expanded from its base in New South Wales and Queensland to become a national competition from 1983, with clubs in the five main Australian cities. Regional clubs, in places such as Canberra, Melbourne, and North Queensland, joined the league. In recent decades, Rugby League has expanded its appeal to encompass white-collar support, and many female supporters have joined what was once as much a male bastion as the Australian pub.

Australian Rules Football is the most distinctively Antipodean ball game that commands wide popularity in Australia. The game was first played between two private schools in Melbourne in the 1850s, and was originally contested with various types of ball, different rules and varied durations. It was played in Victoria, South Australia, Queensland, and Tasmania by the 1860s, and soon after spread to Western Australia. The rules and format of the game were changed and refined under the auspices of the Victorian Football Association, and then the breakaway Victorian Football League, founded in 1896. Originally an amateur game, professionalism was legalized in 1911. 'Aussie Rules' has always had a strong following in Melbourne and its suburbs, and it is still a major spectator sport. Until the 1960s, it was common for players to have a part-time commitment to the game. From the 1970s onwards, the sport has become fully professional, with television rights and corporate funding providing more revenue than gate receipts. In that sense, it has followed a similar trajectory to the professionalization and commercialization of other ball games in Australia.

Aussie Rules football (colloquially called 'footy') has provided exciting entertainment for the rivalries between Melbourne suburbs such as Carlton, Hawthorn, Collingwood, St Kilda, and others. Arthur Streeton's painting of one such contest was entitled *The National Game* (1889), suggesting the sport's broad appeal. Crowds have often been large, well into the thousands. Even in the Depression years of the inter-war period, the Grand Final at the end of each season attracted over 100,000 spectators. As the game became fully professional in the 1980s, it spread its net to incorporate interstate clubs. In 1982, the South Melbourne Club moved to the Sydney Cricket Ground to become the Sydney Swans, and more recently clubs such as the West Coast Eagles (in Perth), Adelaide, and the Brisbane Bears (later Lions) have competed in the annual competition. The Australian Football League now oversees the game. Unlike the two versions of rugby, played on a rectangular pitch, Australian Rules football is played on an oval with 18 players.

The first known cricket match in Australia occurred at Sydney in 1803. The sport gained popularity by the 1830s and, unlike in England, the middle classes often played working-class teams. The first intercolonial games were played between New South Wales and Victoria; then South Australia and Queensland joined. Western Australia and Tasmania formed teams after the Second World War. Today, the main domestic competition is the Sheffield Shield, established in 1892/3 and competed for by the six individual states. At national level, Australia has had a Test cricket team since the 1870s. Every year, the team plays international test matches, usually lasting five days, against England and Commonwealth countries such as New Zealand, South Africa, India, Pakistan, and the West Indies. Test matches are keenly contested. Those between England and Australia, usually held every three or four years on an alternating basis in each country, are keenly anticipated by cricket lovers and attract extensive media coverage. England and Australia compete for 'the Ashes', the burnt remains in an urn of a cricket bail used in a test match in 1882.

Many Australian cricketers have found fame, none more so than Sir Donald Bradman in the 1930s and 1940s, a batsman whose career record far surpasses anyone else. Over the past 30 years, cricket has become more commercialized and somewhat removed from its gentlemanly origins. Shorter contests, confined to one day, have attracted large crowds. Cricket achieved controversial status in the early 1930s when the English team visiting Australia were involved in the 'Bodyline' tour of 1932–3. During those tests, the England paceman Harold Larwood proved almost unplayable by bowling very fast, short deliveries so that they bounced steeply off the pitch to target the batsman's body. This became an international incident. Australia's captain Bill Woodfull explained the situation to the England manager Pelham Warner: 'I don't want to see you Mr. Warner. There are two teams out there; one is trying to play cricket and the other is not.' Controversy of a different kind caused headlines in cricket in the late 1970s when

8. Melbourne cricket ground

the Australian entrepreneur Kerry Packer promoted one-day cricket contests and four-day games for a mass television audience embracing a more commercialized version of the game.

Horseracing has long been a popular sport in Australia. It was always associated with betting. The Melbourne Cup is Australia's most famous thoroughbred horserace. Begun in 1861, it is held on the first Tuesday in November at Flemington racecourse. Known as the race that stops a nation, it attracts the attention of most

Australians and is always televised. Those living in metropolitan Melbourne have a day's holiday to enjoy the race. The most famous winner of the cup was Phar Lap, a New Zealand-bred horse, in 1930. This horse had to be kept in hiding until an hour before the race after an attempt to shoot him. The first automatic totalizator on cup day operated in 1931. Today, the Melbourne Cup has six million Australian dollars in prize money.

Most popular sports played in Australia attract widespread gambling, either legal or illegal. Gambling existed at sporting occasions by the 1820s, mainly with regard to racing, but also in relation to cricket and prizefighting. In Sydney, by the 1830s, a sporting sub-culture existed in which gambling was an integral part of the entertainment. Groups of men known as 'the fancy' or 'the sporting world' earned a living through betting. The first 'bookie' on a Sydney racecourse appeared in 1857. By the late 19th century, newspaper advertising, the emergence of a specialist sporting press, and 'form' guides influenced decisions made by gamblers. Totalizators became commonplace in New South Wales and Victoria by the 1920s and 1930s. In those decades, gambling was boosted by radio advertising and by licensed betting shops. The commercialization of sport through gambling was a controversial issue, with temperance groups, Protestant nonconformists, and female activists often opposed to something they perceived as socially evil and closely connected with alcohol, fecklessness, and violence among working-class gamblers. But the amount of revenue generated by gambling via taxes became an important source of funds for state governments. Today, TAB agencies are a common feature in Australia, and most hotels and inns have gambling machines attached to them.

Art

Aboriginal paintings, on cave walls or barks of trees, were undertaken for thousands of years before Europeans arrived in Australia. Ancient examples of such art survive in Arnhem Land in the Northern Territory. Aboriginal art makes extensive use of ancestral designs and symbols for waterholes, rainbows, fire or smoke, often coupled to powerful stories about the human relationship to the land and the soil's sacred qualities. Such paintings often depicted what Europeans referred to as 'the Dreaming' – the sustaining stories about the world's creation and mankind's relationship with the natural and spiritual world based on the handing down of memories from one generation to the next. The Rainbow Serpent was a commonly used symbol in Aboriginal paintings to depict an important creator figure who was the guardian of sacred places. Interpretation of such symbols was not intended to be easy for the uninitiated. Thus, contemporary Central and Western Desert Art uses dots, prominent in Papunya painting, as a way of hiding sacred features of Aboriginal customs from non-Indigenous people. Aboriginal art benefited from cooperative studios, with state support, that emerged shortly after Aborigines were granted citizenship in Australia. Such art has now become popular with tourists. Widely displayed throughout Australia and admired internationally, it often carries a political content. This is evident in a painting such as Christopher Pease's *Hunting Party* (2003), which shows European explorers overriding the spiritual beliefs of the Nyoongar people's relationship to the wetlands and river systems of King George Sound, Western Australia.

The first non-Indigenous artists in Australia sailed with the voyages of discovery under Cook and Flinders. Sydney Parkinson, the artist on the *Endeavour* (1770), and Ferdinand Bauer, the artist on the *Investigator* (1802–3), both made realistic drawings of Australian plants and animals. Artists in colonial Australia, usually trained in Europe, painted the landscape, Indigenous people, and flora and fauna. The best-known artist of this period was Joseph Lycett, a former transported convict, whose *Views in Australia* (1825) were the largest and most accomplished aquatints and etchings of New South Wales and Van Diemen's Land before the gold rush. Lycett's paintings were firmly in a pastoral tradition that combined imagination with reality; they portrayed Australia as a landscape of agricultural settlement and gardens, and in doing so were partly geared towards how a British art market wished to see Australia. Lycett's depiction of Aboriginal groups was often central to his paintings. Indigenous people were also painted by John Glover, a British emigrant to Australia. His *Mount Wellington and Hobart Town from Kangaroo Point* (c. 1834), however, depicted the landscape of Van Diemen's Land as if it were the English Lake District. One of the most accurate paintings of the Australian bush was the Austrian emigrant Eugene von Guérard's *Ferntree Gully in the Dandenong Ranges* (1857), which was such a popular depiction of the giant, sombre ferns that the location became a picnic site for weekend excursions. That the painting had been done in a Melbourne studio rather than *en plein air* had little effect on these visits.

A more distinctively Australian school of painting emerged in the 1880s and 1890s in the work of Tom Roberts, Charles Conder, Frederick McCubbin, and Arthur Streeton. Influenced by European impressionism and by the pride surrounding the centenary of white settlement in Australia in 1888, they wanted to develop 'what we believe will be a great school of painting in Australia'. They painted everyday scenes that depicted characteristic features of the Australian landscape with figures that were portrayed as typical Australians. In that sense, these painters were involved in projecting mythical figures to some extent. A good example is Roberts's *Shearing the Rams* (1890), a large oil painting with masculine, strong labourers toiling away at a typically Australian occupation. Roberts wanted to convey the feeling of 'evening in the bush and feeling the delight and fascination of the great pastoral life and work…the whole lit warm with the reflection of Australian sunlight'.

McCubbin's paintings often concentrated on portrayals of typical figures that settled Australia's colonies. In the *Pioneer* (1904), he painted three stages in the life of a selector and his wife in the bush – their arrival on the land, their settling there, and their

9. *Shearing the Rams*, by Tom Roberts (1890)

grave. Streeton's paintings show the brilliant summer light and blue skies on a sun-parched Australia, with emphasis on lonely pioneer achievements in the bush. *The Selectors' Hut* (1890), with its lonely figure straddled across a log, with a modest hut and a single, tall eucalypt behind him, set against a background of sun and aridity, is a classic example of this style of painting.

Australian art of the 20th century depicted the landscape in different ways. George Lambert's *The Squatter's Daughter* (1932–4) presented a leisurely, harmonious view of the bush, with a smartly dressed woman pausing with her horse to admire the land surrounding her. A highly divergent view of the Australian landscape is represented in Margaret Preston's *Flying over the Shoalhaven River* (1942), which adopts a perspective taken from above the clouds and focuses on a landscape coloured drably with brown, white, and ochre, with dotted applications reminiscent of Indigenous bark painting. This was one of the first paintings in which a white Australian artist incorporated painting techniques used by Aborigines. Russell Drysdale's paintings, such as *The*

Drover's Wife (1945), continued to depict quintessential Australian bush figures, but conveyed a mysterious sense of the timeless force of nature. Sidney Nolan's series of paintings based on the career of the bushranger Ned Kelly, completed in 1946–7, strongly portrayed an iconic anti-establishment Australian figure dauntlessly bestriding the landscape.

Literature

The first distinctive Australian literature arose in the late 19th century, with the work of the poets Henry Lawson and 'Banjo' Paterson. Lawson depicted the bush as a harsh, bleak, lonely environment, but Paterson had a more optimistic view, referring to the outback as 'the vision splendid of the sunlit plains extended'. Paterson's *Clancy of the Overthrow*, the tale of a Queensland drover, and *The Man from Snowy River*, the story of a horseback pursuit to recapture the colt of a prizewinning racehorse, are classic poems of bushmen on the frontier. Paterson was also the author of Australia's unofficial national anthem, 'Waltzing Matilda', in which the jauntiness of the tune is set beside the sombre tale of the swagman who steals a sheep and jumps into a billabong (a small oxbow lake) to commit suicide rather than being caught by the stockman and troopers. Lawson's grim view of the bush and its hardships, conveyed sardonically, can be discerned in his *Up from the Country*, *The City Bushman*, and *Freedom on the Wallaby*, as well as in his spare prose stories collected in *While the Billy Boils* (1896).

The next generation of Australian writers also made use of specifically Australian themes for their prose and verse. Miles Franklin's novel *My Brilliant Career* (1901) is an ironic and sad tale of dashed hopes in rural New South Wales. Henry Handel Richardson's *The Fortunes of Richard Mahony*, originally published as three separate novels and then as a trilogy in 1930, draws upon the life of her father, a doctor in Victoria. C. J. Dennis wrote popular verse that reflected Australia's contribution to the

First World War. This is epitomized by his *The Moods of Ginger Mick* (1916), which recounts Ginger's brave deeds during the conflict and his death at Gallipoli; this is a sequel to his verse novel *The Sentimental Bloke* (1916). Both poems include liberal doses of Australian slang. The pioneering aspects of Australian history were the backdrop for colourful, popular books written by Ion Idriess, including *Lasseter's Last Ride* (1931), *The Desert Column* (1932), and *Over the Range* (1937). These books dealt respectively with the gold discovery in Australia's centre, the Australian Light Horsemen at Gallipoli, and Aborigines in the Kimberley. Australian poets were slow to explore the experiences of Indigenous people until the appearance of verse by Judith Wright after the Second World War.

Some Australian writers became expatriates. Their writings often combined attachment to their new environment (usually England) with an undertow of Australian content. Martin Boyd's Langton quartet of novels, written in the decade after 1952, fall into this category. In more recent times, Australian expatriate writers have included gifted poets such as Peter Porter, controversial feminist writers such as Germaine Greer, maverick journalists and television critics such as Clive James, and art critics such as Robert Hughes. None of these authors wrote from an exclusively Australian perspective, but they frequently projected their Australian-ness as part of their literary and intellectual identity.

In 1939, the poet A. D. Hope marked a distinctive break with the Australian literary past in his *Australia*, which challenged the oft-repeated view of Australia as a cultural wasteland compared with the richness of European culture. Instead, Hope suggested that Australia, taken on its own terms, could offer cultural enrichment 'if still from the deserts the prophets come'. Since 1945, Australia has produced writers of international renown who have gained deserved reputations for the quality of their imaginative work. Thomas Keneally has combined writing on

Australian historical themes with novels exploring universal moral themes. *Schindler's Ark* (1982), based on recollections of the Holocaust, is probably his best-known work. Peter Carey's novels have an international readership. Among his books with a specifically Australian focus is the *True History of the Kelly Gang* (2001), a depiction of the brutal life of the Victorian bushranger which won the Man Booker Prize in 2001. The writer with the best claim to recognition as a great Australian novelist is the late Patrick White, who explored inner worlds as well as outer events. He wrote twelve completed novels, including *Voss* (1957) and *The Eye of the Storm* (1973). He was awarded the Nobel Prize for Literature in 1973.

Music

Music was everywhere in colonial Australia. Musical instruments arrived with the First Fleet and the military corps in early New South Wales had regimental bands. In the bush, ballads about the lives of convicts, bushrangers, and drovers were commonly sung. Choral singing became a mainstay in the large cities from the 1830s onwards, with *liedertafel*, associated particularly with German immigrant groups, spreading in Adelaide, Brisbane, Sydney, and Melbourne. Most Australian middle-class homes had a piano by the middle of the 19th century. Visiting opera companies, many with European singers promoted by European impresarios, were common in the large cities. Amateur orchestras formed in the colonial capitals from the 1860s onwards. Notable singers emerged, such as the soprano Nellie Melba and the bass-baritone Peter Dawson, who performed regularly at Europe's main musical venues but also retained their attachment to Australia. Large international exhibitions held in Melbourne in 1880-1 and 1888 and in Hobart in 1894-5 assembled expert orchestras and choral societies that were well attended and whetted the public's appreciation of music. Orchestras founded by G. W. L. Marshall-Hall in Melbourne and Heinrich Heinicke in Adelaide during the 1890s, and later by Henri Verbrugghen in

Sydney during the First World War, indicated the potentially high standards of orchestral music-making possible in Australia.

However, professionalization in music in Australia occurred gradually. One drawback to its quicker development lay in the lack of private, state and federal patronage for music. In addition, demand had to be generated among Australians for finer music. The Australian Broadcasting Commission (ABC), founded in 1932, was a central institutional organization for creating and sustaining this demand by broadcasting serious and lighter music and by supporting dance bands and radio orchestras. The latter were upgraded to full symphony orchestras in the immediate post-Second World War era. Between 1945 and 1951, the Sydney Symphony, the Victorian Symphony (now the Melbourne Symphony), the South Australian Symphony (now the Adelaide Symphony), the Tasmanian Symphony, the Queensland Symphony, and the West Australian Symphony orchestras were formed through partnerships between the ABC and the municipal and state governments. These orchestras have survived until today as important cultural ambassadors for their cities and states. Each year, they play varied programmes of classical music, interspersed with jazz, swing, and 'crossover' music, to many thousands of Australians and international visitors.

In more recent years, a specialist smaller ensemble, the Australian Chamber Orchestra, has invigorated Australia's cultural scene, presenting programmes that offer an eclectic mix of standard classical works, arrangement of chamber compositions, and newly commissioned works. The Australian Chamber Orchestra undertakes regular tours throughout Australia and overseas. Chamber music has also been catered for in Australia by the activities of Musica Viva, which has sponsored string quartet recitals and other chamber ensembles since the 1940s. Today, groups such the Australia Ensemble, based at the University of New South Wales, and Southern Cross Soloists, continue this tradition.

Opera developed more slowly in Australia. Popular operas by Bizet and Verdi were performed in Australian cities in the late 19th century. W. S. Lyster's company mounted the first Australian production of Wagner's *Ring* cycle in Sydney just before the First World War. Dame Nellie Melba became an internationally renowned Australian opera singer, a great supporter of musical life in Australia and, latterly, famous for seemingly never-ending farewell concerts. But opera was expensive to stage, and a paucity of trained singers, instrumentalists and lack of financial patronage meant that it was an occasional affair in Australia until the Second World War. Matters improved markedly with the formation of the Elizabethan Theatre Trust, which gave more regular performances of opera from the mid-1950s onwards. This body, supported by federal funds, was important in launching the career of Australia's internationally renowned soprano Joan Sutherland (known as 'La Stupenda' for the brilliance, range, and tonal accuracy of her voice). But opera in Australia only really came of age when the Sydney Opera House opened its doors for the first time in 1973. Situated at Bennelong Point, near Circular Quay, Sydney, and instantly recognizable as a symbol of Australia throughout the world, this building of egg shells piled together resulted from a long gestation and brought its Danish architect, Jørn Utzon, world renown. Though controversial for having a larger concert hall than an opera theatre – the two auditoria in the building were originally intended for each other's purpose – this has become the home of Opera Australian.

Australia's classical composers took a long time to find a distinctively Australian voice. Until the 1940s, the only Australian composer who had made an international reputation was the idiosyncratic Percy Grainger, a pianist of international standard and composer of music more inspired by English folk songs than Australian themes. Australia's classical composers by that time had a very low profile. The years since the Second World War have been notable for greater exposure of Australian compositions to broader audiences, helped by the commitment of the ABC towards programming Australian music and the circulation of recorded studio performances. Major composers have emerged. One is the Tasmanian Peter Sculthorpe, whose music is inspired by Australia's contrasting landscapes. Another was Richard Meale, whose music often took Australia's history and literature as its starting point. His opera *Voss* – the most accomplished Australian opera yet written – depicts the lonely journey of the explorer Ludwig Leichhardt through central Australia from a libretto based on Patrick White's novel. With notable individual exceptions, however, Australian compositions have garnered relatively little attention beyond the southern hemisphere except when played by visiting Australian artists, composers and ensembles.

Australian popular music has varied styles and traditions. The oldest form of popular music stems from Aboriginal customs and practices, notably the ceremonial Corroboree practised at gatherings of Indigenous people. Aboriginal instruments such as the didgeridoo are easily recognized by non-Indigenous audiences. The Australian composer John Antill wrote a ballet called *Corroboree* based on Aboriginal themes. The full ballet was first performed in 1950. The didgeridoo player William Barton has collaborated in music that mixes Aboriginal and classical traditions. He is on record as saying that he wants to 'take the oldest culture in the world and blend it with Europe's rich musical legacy'. Barton was the soloist in Sculthorpe's *Requiem* (2004), a work for didgeridoo, chorus, and orchestra premiered at the Adelaide Festival of the Arts in 2004. But it is the group Yothu Yindi who have made the main bridge between Aboriginal and mainstream music in their song 'Treaty' from their album *Tribal Voice* (1991).

Australia also has had many other forms of popular music, including country, rhythm and blues, rock and roll, jazz, folk, and pop, all of which have strong followings in clubs and at outdoor festivals. The most successful Australian popular singer was Slim

Dusty, who rose to fame in the 1950s, adapted US country music to Australian idioms and achieved more than seven million record sales. Some Australian popular music performers have achieved international success, including groups such as the Shadows and the Bee Gees, and solo singers such as Kylie Minogue; other Australian popular musicians have had more success within Australia itself, such as the singer John Farnham.

Conclusion

Australia was the last inhabitable continent explored by Europeans. For centuries, theoretical geographers and maritime explorers tried to locate Terra Australis Incognita, but the first landing there by a European did not occur until the early 17th century. Colonization in the Antipodes began in 1788 with the arrival of the First Fleet. Beginning as a small convict outpost in the southeastern corner of the continent, centred on Sydney and its hinterland, settlement in Australia expanded rapidly during the 19th century. Six colonies were founded. Free settlers were attracted in large numbers with assisted passage schemes from the 1830s onwards. The gold rush of the 1850s drew thousands of immigrants down under. A burgeoning economy, originally based on limited domestic demand, expanded during the 19th century to become intertwined with an international economy through exports of wool, gold, other minerals, wheat, and eventually refrigerated meat and butter. These commodities were mainly shipped to Europe in return for the manufactured products of that continent. Though there were economic depressions in the early 1840s and during the 1890s, Australia's colonies experienced considerable economic growth in the 19th century.

During the convict era, Australia's colonies lacked parliaments or elected politicians for the most part. Matters changed rapidly, however, after Britain granted responsible government to the Australian colonies in 1852. The gold rush era witnessed the establishment of colonial parliaments and extensive voting rights for men and women. Liberal reform measures were championed. Trade unionism flourished for many skilled workers from the middle of the 19th century. The Australian colonies became known as places of opportunity for the working classes of Britain and Ireland, a working man's paradise in the southern hemisphere. After the gold rush era, more and more settlers were Australian-born and were proud of their native country. Though they regarded themselves as Queenslanders or Victorians or South Australians, by the 1890s they realized the advantages that would emerge, politically and economically, if they were to combine together in a formal union. The coming of Federation in 1901 established Australia as a nation in which political power would operate at both a federal and state level.

During the 20th century, Australia's staple exports maintained their strong place in international trade, and mineral resources and exports, along with new overseas markets in Asian countries, helped to develop and diversify the Australian economy. Manufacturing rose from being a relatively modest sector in economic life to a more important part of the economy, as greater industrialization occurred from the Second World War onwards. Automobiles, chemicals, iron and steel, electricity, and electronic equipment all grew rapidly in Australia after 1945. Banks, insurance businesses, and other financial institutions proliferated over the course of the 20th century, providing Australians with the business resources appropriate for a modern, economically developed nation. That these banks were strongly regulated helped Australia to escape many of the fiscal woes of the global economic crisis of the early 21st century. Australia's economy now has an important service sector covering retail, tourism, entertainment, health, education, IT, and telecommunications.

Political development after Federation saw the emergence of political parties at state and federal level, the creation of the office of prime minister, the use of courts for industrial arbitration, the introduction of sophisticated voting procedures for elections, and the growth of Canberra and the Australian Capital Territory as the seat of federal parliamentary government. Australia remains constitutionally tied to Britain in 2012, with the monarch of the United Kingdom as the official head of state. But this is largely a nominal role. In most respects, Australians are responsible for their own political affairs. After maintaining a fairly modest military role during the 19th century, Australia developed an army, navy, and air force in the 20th century, fought in both World Wars, and contributed to subsequent conflicts in Korea and Vietnam. Relying mainly on British military help until the Second World War, Australia has since become more aligned with diplomatic and military support from the United States. Contemporary Australian diplomacy and foreign policy seeks to maintain stable political and economic relations with Asian neighbours. All recent governments, however, have treated Australia's alliance with the United States as the centrepiece of its foreign policy.

The original inhabitants of Australia, the Aborigines, have struggled during the past two centuries. Colonized by Europeans who understood little of their culture and spiritual connections with the land, Aborigines faced severe effects of diseases such as smallpox during the early decades of contact with settlers. This led to extensive Aboriginal deaths. Although many instances of cooperation occurred between Indigenous people and colonizers, Aboriginal lands were overrun, violence occurred on the pastoral frontier, and Indigenous people became marginalized in numbers and in their stake in Australian society. When Australia became a nation, Aborigines were excluded from the vote, from citizenship, and from the census. During the 20th century, 'stolen generations' of Aboriginal children were removed from their families. Only with the greater racial awareness from the 1960s onwards did

Aborigines improve their situation. By 1962, most restrictions on Aborigines voting at elections had been rescinded. A 1967 national referendum voted overwhelmingly to have Aborigines included in the census. But today, although Indigenous land claims have the backing of the Mabo and Wik judgments, Aboriginal communities separated from mainstream Australia are beset with problems of disease, alcoholism, and abuse.

The social and cultural transformation of Australia since c. 1950 has been rapid and substantial. Until then, Australia was largely an Anglo-Celtic enclave in the southern hemisphere, drawing its political and cultural traditions mainly from Britain and Ireland, staunchly defending a 'White Australia Policy', and strongly connected to its European roots. Australia is largely an urban nation, in terms of population distribution, but the imaginative lure of the outback, with its emphasis on independence, mateship, and egalitarianism, has left a strong imprint. Since 1950, the decline and eventual demise of the 'White Australia Policy', the large influx of Continental Europeans and, later, Asian immigrants, the greater awareness and promotion of multiculturalism, the decline of Australia's economic connections with Britain, and the recognition that Australia's chief diplomatic and commercial interests lie in China, Japan, and other Asian countries rather than in Britain, Ireland, or the European Union, have transformed the Australian nation. Australia today is a thriving, peaceful, multicultural democracy, with strong economic, political, and diplomatic connections with the Asia-Pacific region. Whether Australia will eventually cut the umbilical cord with its British roots and become a republic is yet to be decided.

Timeline

1606 March	Willem Janszoon in the *Duyken* reaches the Cape York peninsula. The first recorded landfall by a European on Australian soil.
1642	Dutchman Abel Tasman explores the west coast of Van Diemen's Land.
1688	Englishman William Dampier explores the west coast of Australia.
1770	James Cook on the *Endeavour* charts the east coast of Australia and claims it for the British Crown.
1788	The First Fleet of convicts arrives in Sydney Harbour to begin white settlement in Australia.
1803	Matthew Flinders completes the first circumnavigation of Australia.
1804	The first white settlers arrive in Van Diemen's Land.
1808	The 'Rum' rebellion against Governor William Bligh.
1813	First crossing of the Blue Mountains by settlers.
1824	Permission granted to change the name of the continent from New Holland to Australia.
1825	Van Diemen's Land becomes a colony.
1829	The whole of mainland Australia claimed as British territory.
1829	The Swan River colony founded. Renamed Western Australia in 1832.

1833	Port Arthur founded as a penal settlement in Van Diemen's Land.
1835	A settlement established at Port Phillip, now Melbourne.
1836	South Australia founded as a colony.
1840	Convict transportation ends in New South Wales.
1850	Western Australia becomes a penal colony.
1851	Victoria separates from New South Wales and becomes a colony.
1851	The Victorian gold rush starts.
1854	The Eureka stockade, Ballarat, Victoria.
1856	Van Diemen's Land becomes Tasmania.
1859	Queensland separates from New South Wales and becomes a colony.
1861	The Burke and Wills expedition.
1868	End of convict transportation to Western Australia.
1873	Uluru first sighted by Europeans and named Ayer's Rock.
1877	First England–Australia test match.
1879	First Australian Trade Unions Congress held.
1880	The bushranger Ned Kelly is hanged.
1890	Australian Federation Conference calls a constitutional convention.
1901 1 January	Australia becomes a federated nation, known as the Commonwealth of Australia.
1903	The High Court of Australia established.
1911	The Northern Territory comes under Commonwealth control, being removed from the control of South Australia.
1911	The Australian Capital Territory established.
1914	Australian soldiers sent to the First World War.
1915 25 April	Australian forces land at Anzac Cove on the Gallipoli peninsula, Turkey.
1927	Opening of the federal Parliament in Canberra, the Australian capital city.
1932	Sydney Harbour Bridge constructed.

1939 September	Australia enters the Second World War.
1945	Australia becomes a founding member of the United Nations.
1949	Construction of the Snowy Mountains hydro-electric scheme begins.
1951	Australia signs the ANZUS Treaty with the United States and New Zealand.
1962	Commonwealth Electoral Act gives Indigenous Australians the right to enrol and vote at federal elections.
1966	Decimalization introduced.
1973	The Sydney Opera House opens.
1988	Australia celebrates its bicentenary.
1992	High Court delivers the Mabo decision, which rules that native title exists.
1996	High Court hands down the Wik decision, which states that Indigenous native title can withstand the granting of pastoral leases.
1999	A referendum on changing to a republic is unsuccessful.

References

Chapter 1: The making of Australia

Walter Murdoch's quotation is cited in Anna Haebich, 'The Battlefields of Aboriginal History' in Martyn Lyons and Penny Russell (eds.), *Australia's History: Themes and Debates* (Sydney: University of New South Wales Press, 2005), p. 2. F. K. Crowley's remark is quoted in Robert Pascoe, *The Manufacture of Australian History* (Melbourne: Oxford University Press, 1979), p. 107. The quotation by John Campbell comes from his *Navigantium atque Itinerantium Bibliotheca: or, a Compleat Collection of Voyages and Travels*, 2 vols (London, 1744–8), i., p. 65. The first quotation from Cook is in J. C. Beaglehole (ed.), *The Journals of Captain Cook: The Voyage of the Resolution and Discovery, 1776–1780* (Cambridge: Hakluyt Society, Cambridge University Press, 1967), pp. 321–2. For the second quotation by Cook, see J. C. Beaglehole (ed.), *The Journals of Captain James Cook: The Voyage of the Endeavour, 1768–1771* (Cambridge: Hakluyt Society, Cambridge University Press, 1955), p. 399. Hobbles Danaiyarri's narrative is the first chapter in Deryck M. Schreuder and Stuart Ward (eds.), *Australia's Empire* (Oxford: Oxford University Press, 2008). James Mudie's comment is taken from his book *The Felonry of New South Wales: being a faithful picture of the real romance of life in Botany Bay, with anecdotes of Botany Bay Society and a plan of Sydney* (London: Whaley and Co., 1837), pp. 13–14. The 1864 observation on convictism is from K. S. Inglis, *Australian Colonists: An Exploration of Social History, 1788–1870* (Carlton, Vic.: Melbourne University Press, 1993), p. 14. The slogan for Manly as a workers' paradise was coined by the Port Jackson and Manly Steamship Company.

Barton's views on immigration are from his speech on the Immigration Restriction Bill in the House of Representatives *Debates*, 26 September 1901, p. 5233. Deakin's conception of white Australia is found in J. A. La Nauze (ed.), *A. Deakin, Federated Australia: Selections from Letters to the Morning Post, 1900–1910* (Carlton, Vic.: Melbourne University Press, 1968), p. 80. The phrase 'global colour line' is explained in Marilyn Lake and Henry Reynolds, *Drawing the Global Colour Line: White Men's Countries and the International Challenge of Racial Equality* (Cambridge: Cambridge University Press, 2008). The quotation about the demise of white Australia is taken from the title of Gwenda Tavan's *The Long, Slow Death of White Australia* (Carlton North, Vic.: Scribe, 2005).

Chapter 2: Shaping the continent

The phrase 'replenishing the earth' is from James Belich, *Replenishing the Earth: The Settler Revolution and the Rise of the Anglo-World, 1783–1939* (Oxford: Oxford University Press, 2009). 'The tyranny of distance' is another phrase from a book title: Geoffrey Blainey, *The Tyranny of Distance: How Distance Shaped Australian History* (Melbourne: Sun Books, 1966). 'Seaport industrial machine' comes from James Bird, *Seaport Gateways of Australia* (Oxford: Oxford University Press, 1968), p. 139. G. C. Mundy is quoted from his book *Our Antipodes*, 3 vols (London: Richard Bentley, 1852), i, p. 306. The excerpt from the 'Jerilderie Letter' is from Max Brown, *Australian Son: The Story of Ned Kelly* (Melbourne: Georgian House, 1948), p. 282. The quotation from the Polish gold-miner is found in Seweryn Korzelinski, tr. and ed. by Stanley Robe, *Memoirs of Gold-Digging in Australia* (St Lucia: University of Queensland Press, 1979), p. 55. The observer at the gold rush in 1853 was John Sherer, *The Gold-Finder of Australia: how he went, how he fared, and how he made his fortune* (London: Clarke, Beeton, & Co., 1853), p. 10. The comment about the Chinese was published in the *Newsletter of Australasia or Narrative of Events: A Letter to Send to Friends, no. 9* (March 1857). The Webbs' comparison of British and Australian cities is quoted in Lionel Frost, *Australian Cities in Comparative View* (Ringwood, Vic.: McPhee Gribble, 1990), p. 59. The positive view of 'hives of workers' in Australia's cities comes from W. Pember Reeves, *State Experiments in Australia and New Zealand*, 2 vols

(London: Alexander Moring, 1902), i, p. 37. Jevons's remark was reprinted in the *Sydney Morning Herald*, 7 December 1929. 'The New Urban Frontier' is discussed in Lionel Frost, *The New Urban Frontier: Urbanisation and City Building in Australasia and the American West* (Kensington, NSW: University of New South Wales Press, 1991). 'Marvellous Melbourne' was a phrase originally coined by an English journalist on a visit to Melbourne in 1885: see George Augustus Sala, *The Life and Adventures of George Augustus Sala*, 2 vols (London: Cassell, 1895), ii, p. 423. The 1883 description of Melbourne appears in R. E. N. Twopeny, *Town Life in Australia* (London: Elliot Stock, 1883), p. 2.

Chapter 3: Governing Australia

Macquarie's view of convicts was expressed in a letter to Bathurst, 28 June 1813, in Frederick Watson (ed.), *Historical Records of Australia*, series 1 (Sydney: Library Committee of the Commonwealth Parliament, 1914–25), vii, pp. 775–6. The Lang quotation is reprinted in Ian Turner (ed.), *The Australian Dream* (Melbourne: Sun Books, 1968). Louisa Lawson's comment on men's dominance in the world is part of her editorial for *The Dawn: A Journal for Australian Women*, October 1890. The quotation on female suffrage in South Australia is part of the South Australian (Female Suffrage) Act, 1895 (available at http://www.foundingdocs.gov.au)

The term 'femocrat' was coined by Hester Eisenstein, *Inside Agitators: Australian Femocrats and the State* (Philadelphia: Temple University Press, 1996). Henry Parkes's speech in favour of Federation is included in his book *The Federal Government of Australia: Speeches Delivered on Various Occasions, November 1889–May 1890* (Sydney: Turner and Henderson, 1890), p. 39. Menzies's praise of the Australian middle classes was part of his radio speech 'The Forgotten People' (1942), included in the Menzies Virtual Museum (http://www.menziesvirtualmuseum.org. au). The first quote from John Howard is from his speech given at the 1997 Reconciliation Convention in Melbourne, 27 May 1997. The second quote from Howard is from the Australian House of Representatives' Motion of Reconciliation, 26 August 1999, p. 9205. Julia Gillard's comment on working towards an Australian republic is taken from *The Sydney Morning Herald*, 17 August 2010.

Chapter 4: Australia and the world

The comment on the impact on Australia of Japan's naval defeat of
Russia in 1905 is quoted in Charles Grimshaw, 'Australian
Nationalism and the Imperial Connection, 1900–14', *Australian
Journal of Politics and History*, 3 (1957–8): 177. McIlwraith's
remark made in 1883 is quoted in W. K. Hancock, *Australia*
(London, 1930), p. 207. 'Our last man and our last shilling' is
found in numerous places, including Neville Meaney (ed.),
*Australia and the World: A Documentary History from the 1870s
to the 1970s* (Melbourne: Longman Cheshire, 1985), p. 217. The
comment on the AIF leaving Sydney to fight in the First World
War is from *The Sydney Morning Herald*, 14 November 1914.
Latham's remark is quoted in Neville Meaney, *Towards a New
Vision: Australia and Japan through 100 Years* (East Roseville,
NSW: Kangaroo Press, 1999), p. 76. The first quotation by Menzies
was published in *The Sydney Morning Herald* on 27 April 1939.
For a transcription of Menzies's radio speech at the beginning of
the Second World War, see the Menzies Virtual Museum website
(http://www.menziesvirtualmuseum.org.au/1930s/).
Curtin's landmark speech of 7 December 1941 was summarized in the
Herald (Melbourne), 27 December 1941. 'The Brisbane Line' was a
phrase coined by MacArthur at a press conference in December
1943. R. S. Ryan's pithy remark of 9 May 1950 on Australia's allies
is recorded in the *Commonwealth Parliamentary Debates*, vol. 207,
p. 2251. Menzies's observation on Vietnam is found in the
Commonwealth Parliamentary Debates, 29 April 1965, p. 120.
Holt's quip on Australian support for the USA is widely reprinted:
see, for example, Frank G. Clarke, *Australia in a Nutshell: A
Narrative History* (Dural Delivery Centre, NSW: Rosenberg, 2003),
p. 278. Gorton's comment on Australian–American relations, made
on 6 May 1969, comes in a speech transcribed on the American
Presidency Project website (http://www.presidency.ucsb.edu/ws/).
Keating's adamant refutation that Australia can ever be a wholly
Asian nation is found in his book *Engagement: Australia Faces the
Asia-Pacific* (Sydney: Macmillan, 2000), pp. 20–1.

Chapter 5: Body and soul

The quotation about Australians as beachgoers is from Robert Drewe
(ed.), *The Picador Book of the Beach* (Sydney: Pan Macmillan,

1993), p. 7. Albert Tucker's remark is quoted in Geoffrey Blainey, *A History of Victoria* (Cambridge: Cambridge University Press, 2006), p. 217. The term 'cultural cringe' was coined by the Melbourne critic and social commentator A. A. Phillips in 1950: see his *The Australian Tradition: Essays in Colonial Culture* (Melbourne: Melbourne University Press, 1958). Woodfull's reaction to the Bodyline controversy is from http://adbonline.anu. edu.au/biogs/A12067b.html. The aims of the Heidelberg painters are summarized in the letter by Tom Roberts, Charles Conder, and Arthur Streeton to the *Argus*, 3 September 1889. Roberts's remark on *Shearing the Rams* was originally included in a letter to the editor of the *Argus*, 4 July 1890. 'The vision splendid' is a quote from Paterson's poem *Clancy of the Overthrow*. William Barton's comment was printed in *The Age*, 9 May 2005.

Further reading

General

Alan Atkinson, *The Europeans in Australia: A History*, 2 vols (Melbourne: Oxford University Press, 1997).

Geoffrey Blainey, *The Tyranny of Distance: How Distance Shaped Australia's History*, revised edn. (South Melbourne: Sun Books, 1983).

David Day, *Claiming a Continent: A New History of Australia* (Sydney: HarperCollins, 1996).

Stuart Macintyre, *A Concise History of Australia*, 3rd edn. (Cambridge: Cambridge University Press, 2010).

John Rickard, *Australia: A Cultural History* (Melbourne: Longman, 1988).

Frank Welsh, *Great Southern Land: A New History of Australia* (London: Allen Lane, 2004).

Chapter 1: The making of Australia

Richard Broome, *Aboriginal Australians*, 3rd edn. (Crows Nest, NSW: Allen & Unwin, 2002).

W. K. Hancock, *Australia*, reprint edn. (Brisbane: Jacaranda Press, 1961).

John Hirst, *Freedom on the Fatal Shore: Australia's First Colony* (Melbourne: Black, 2008).

Robert Hughes, *The Fatal Shore: A History of the Transportation of Convicts to Australia, 1787–1868* (London: Collins Harvill, 1987).

Henry Reynolds, *The Other Side of the Frontier: Aboriginal Resistance to the European Invasion of Australia*, reprint edn. (Kensington, NSW: University of New South Wales Press, 2006).

Eric Richards, *Destination Australia: Migration to Australia since 1901* (Sydney: University of New South Wales Press, 2008).

Chapter 2: Shaping the continent

James Belich, *Replenishing the Earth: The Settler Revolution and the Rise of the Anglo-World, 1783–1939* (Oxford: Oxford University Press, 2009).

Geoffrey Bolton, *Spoils and Spoilers: A History of Australians Shaping Their Environment*, 2nd edn. (Sydney: Allen & Unwin, 1992).

Lionel Frost, *The New Urban Frontier: Urbanisation and City Building in Australasia and the American West* (Kensington, NSW: University of New South Wales Press, 1991).

David Meredith and Barrie Dyster, *Australia and the Global Economy: Continuity and Change* (Cambridge: Cambridge University Press, 1999).

Russel Ward, *The Australian Legend* (Melbourne: Oxford University Press, 1958).

Richard White, *Inventing Australia: Images and Identity, 1688–1980* (Crows Nest, NSW: Allen & Unwin, 1981).

Chapter 3: Governing Australia

Patricia Grimshaw, Marilyn Lake, and Marion Quartly (eds.), *Creating a Nation 1788–2007*, revised edn. (Perth: API Network, Curtin University of Technology, 2006).

John Hirst, *Australia's Democracy: A Short History* (Crows Nest, NSW: Allen & Unwin, 2002).

Helen Irving, *To Constitute a Nation: A Cultural History of Australia's Constitution* (Cambridge: Cambridge University Press, 1997).

Marilyn Lake, *Getting Equal: The History of Australian Feminism* (St Leonards, NSW: Allen & Unwin, 1999).

Mark McKenna, *The Captive Republic: A History of Republicanism in Australia, 1788–1996* (Cambridge: Cambridge University Press, 1996).

Ross McMullin, *The Light on the Hill: The Australian Labor Party, 1891–1991* (Melbourne: Oxford University Press, 1991).

Chapter 4: Australia and the world

David Day, *The Politics of War: Australia at War 1939–45 from Churchill to MacArthur* (Sydney: HarperCollins, 2003).

Jeffrey Grey, *A Military History of Australia*, 3rd edn. (Cambridge: Cambridge University Press, 2008).

T. B. Millar, *Australia in Peace and War: External Relations since 1788*, 2nd edn. (Botany, NSW: Australian National University Press, 1991).

Deryck Schreuder and Stuart Ward (eds.), *Australia's Empire* (Oxford: Oxford University Press, 2008).

David Walker, *Anxious Nation: Australia and the Rise of Asia, 1850–1939* (St Lucia: University of Queensland Press, 1999).

Stuart Ward, *Australia and the British Embrace: The Demise of the Imperial Ideal* (Melbourne: Melbourne University Press, 2001).

Chapter 5: Body and soul

K. S. Inglis, *This is the ABC: The Australian Broadcasting Commission* (Melbourne: Melbourne University Press, 1983).

Peter Pierce (ed.), *The Cambridge History of Australian Literature* (Cambridge: Cambridge University Press, 2009).

Geoffrey Serle, *From Deserts the Prophets Come: The Creative Spirit in Australia, 1788–1972* (Melbourne: Heinemann, 1973).

Bernard Smith with Terry Smith, *Australian Painting: 1788–1990* (Melbourne: Melbourne University Press, 1995).

Richard Waterhouse, *Private Pleasures, Public Leisure: A History of Australian Popular Culture since 1788* (South Melbourne: Longman, 1995).

Wray Vamplew and Brian Stoddart (eds.), *Sport in Australia: A Social History* (Melbourne: Cambridge University Press, 1994).

Index

ONLINE CATALOGUE

Very Short Introductions

Our online catalogue is designed to make it easy to find your ideal Very Short Introduction. View the entire collection by subject area, watch author videos, read sample chapters, and download reading guides.

http://fds.oup.com/www.oup.co.uk/general/vsi/index.html

MODERN CHINA
A Very Short Introduction
Rana Mitter

China today is never out of the news: from human rights controversies and the continued legacy of Tiananmen Square, to global coverage of the Beijing Olympics, and the Chinese 'economic miracle'. It seems a country of contradictions: a peasant society with some of the world's most futuristic cities, heir to an ancient civilization that is still trying to find a modern identity. This *Very Short Introduction* offers the reader with no previous knowledge of China a variety of ways to understand the world's most populous nation, giving a short, integrated picture of modern Chinese society, culture, economy, politics and art.

'A brilliant essay.'

Timothy Garton, TLS

www.oup.com/vsi

MODERN IRELAND
A Very Short Introduction
Senia Paseta

This is a book about the Irish Question, or more specifically about Irish Questions. The term has become something of a catch-all, a convenient way to encompass numerous issues and developments which pertain to the political, social, and economic history of modern Ireland. The Irish Question has of course changed: one of the main aims of this book is to explore the complicated and shifting nature of the Irish Question and to assess what it has meant to various political minds and agendas.

No other issue brought down as many nineteenth-century governments and no comparable twentieth-century dilemma has matched its ability to frustrate the attempts of British cabinets to find a solution; this inability to find a lasting answer to the Irish Question is especially striking when seen in the context of the massive shifts in British foreign policy brought about by two world wars, decolonization, and the cold war.

Senia Paseta charts the changing nature of the Irish Question over the last 200 years, within an international political and social historical context.

www.oup.com/vsi

Modern Japan
A Very Short Introduction
Christopher Goto-Jones

Japan is arguably today's most successful industrial economy, combining almost unprecedented affluence with social stability and apparent harmony. Japanese goods and cultural products are consumed all over the world, ranging from animated movies and computer games all the way through to cars, semiconductors, and management techniques. In many ways, Japan is an icon of the modern world, and yet it remains something of an enigma to many, who see it as a confusing montage of the alien and the familiar, the ancient and modern. The aim of this Very Short Introduction is to explode the myths and explore the reality of modern Japan - by taking a concise look at its history, economy, politics, and culture.

'A wonderfully engaging narrative of a complicated history, which from the beginning to end sheds light on the meaning of modernity in Japan as it changed over time. An exemplary text.'

Carol Gluck, Columbia University